GLORIANA

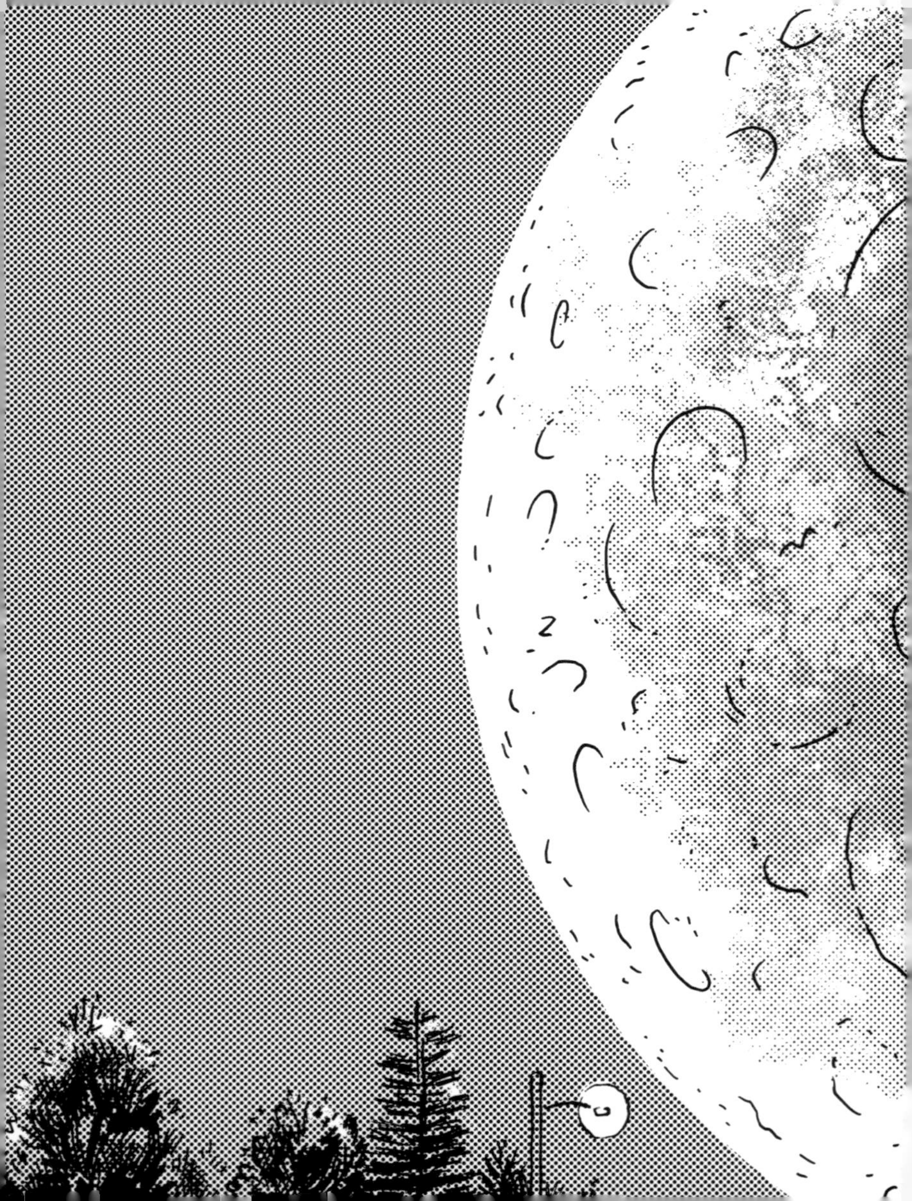

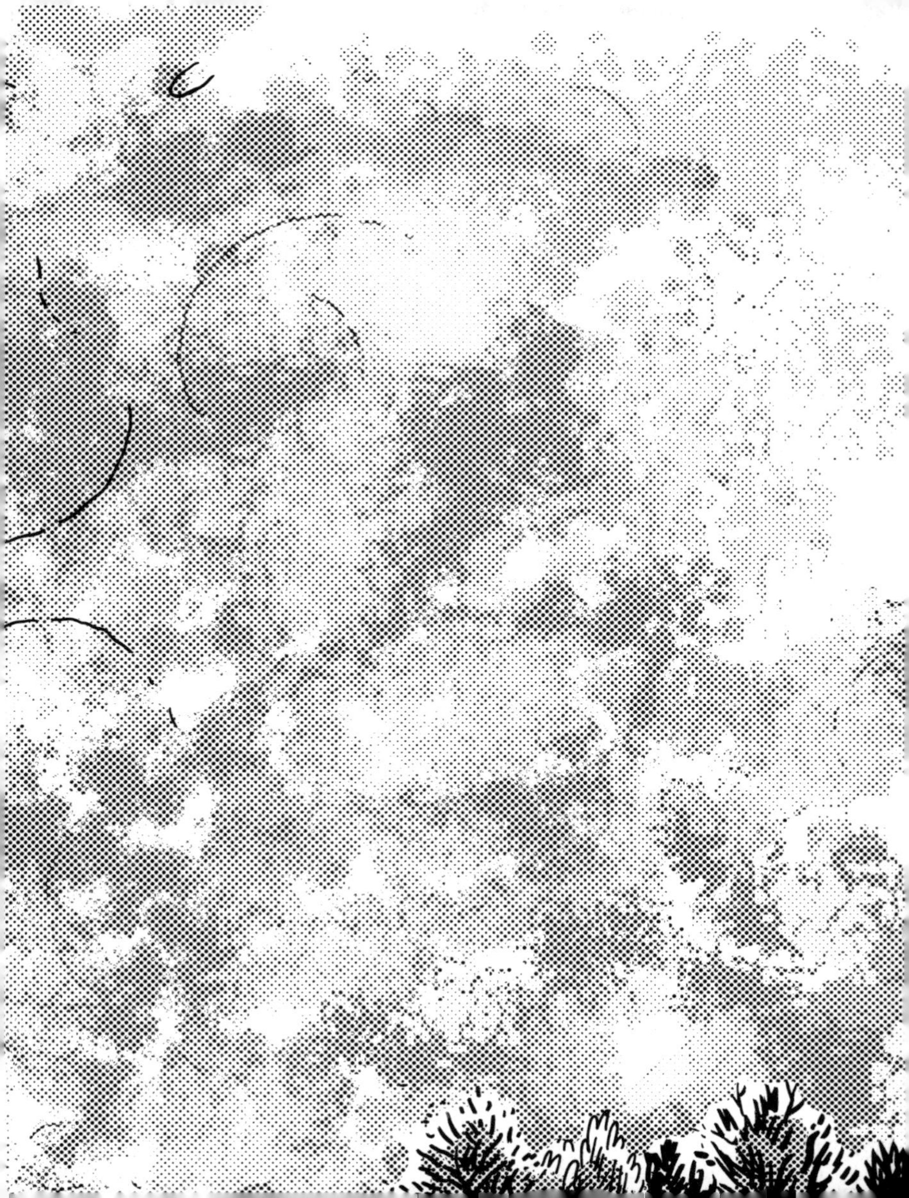

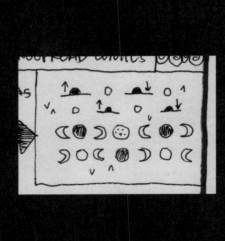

GLORIANA

③ GLENN GANGES
COMICS

GROC.   MOON. ↑
    SUNS. ↓
● PLUS
"Basketball"

BY ⓑ KEVIN H

ORIG.
2001
PUBL.

DRAWN & QUARTERLY   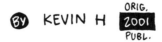   MONTREAL

GLENN GANGES

PUBLICATION INFO

DRAWN & QUARTERLY
POST OFFICE BOX 48056
Montreal, Quebec
Canada H2V 4S8
www.drawnandquarterly.com

First hardcover edition: APRIL 2012
Printed in SINGAPORE
10 9 8 7 6 5 4 3 2 1

Library and Archives
Canada Cataloguing in Publication

Huizenga, Kevin, 1977–
Gloriana / Kevin Huizenga

ISBN 978-1-77046-061-4

I. Title.

PN6727.H8G56 2012
741.5'973
C2011-905289-X

• Distributed in the USA by:
FARRAR, STRAUS and GIROUX
18 West 18th Street
New York, NY 10011
Orders: 888.330.8477

• Distributed in CANADA by:
RAINCOAST BOOKS
2440 Viking Way
Richmond, BC V6V 1N2
Orders: 800-663-5714

• Distributed in the UK by:
PUBLISHERS GROUP UK
8 The Arena, Mollison Avenue
Enfield, EN3 7NL United Kingdom
Orders: 020 8804 0400

FOR GRANDPA HUIZENGA

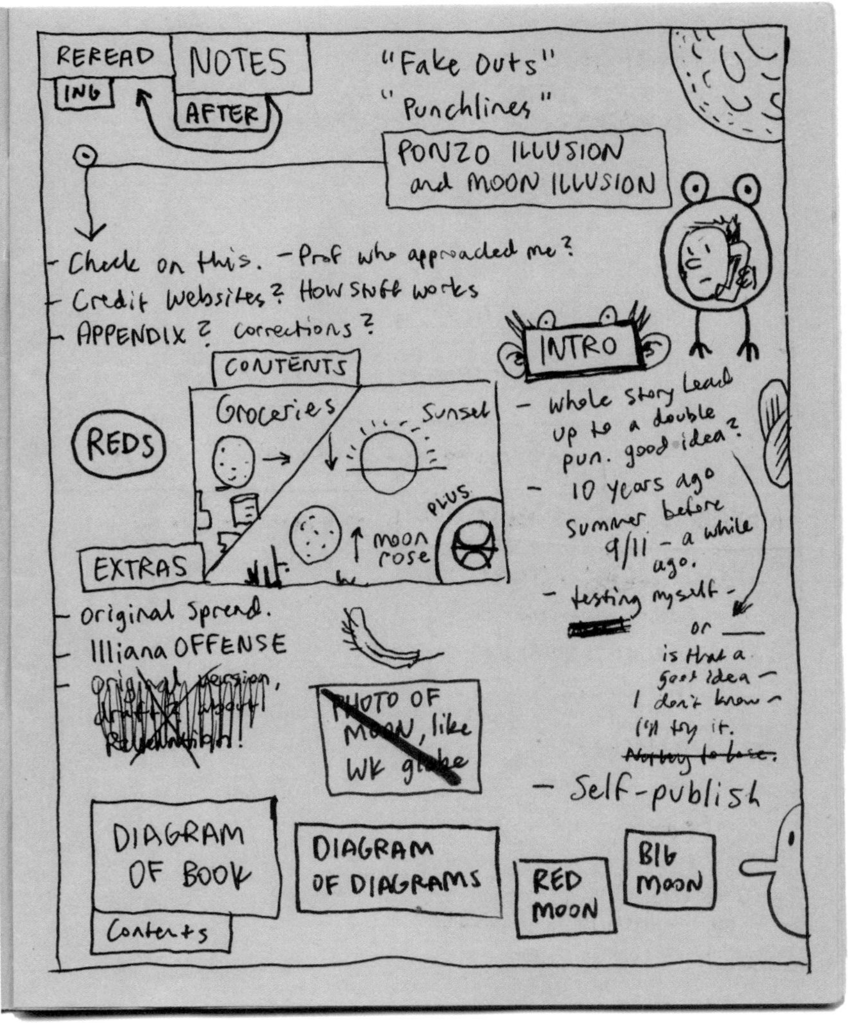
REREAD
ING
NOTES
AFTER
"Fake Outs"
"Punchlines"
PONZO ILLUSION and MOON ILLUSION
- Check on this. - Prof who approached me?
- Credit websites? How stuff works
- APPENDIX? corrections?
INTRO
- whole story lead up to a double pun. good idea?
- 10 years ago summer before 9/11 - a while ago.
- testing myself -
or ___
is that a good idea - I don't know - I'll try it.
Nothing to lose.
- Self-publish
CONTENTS
Groceries
Sunset
PLUS
moon rose
REDS
EXTRAS
- original spread.
- Illiana OFFENSE
- original version,
PHOTO OF MOON, like WK globe
DIAGRAM OF BOOK
Contents
DIAGRAM OF DIAGRAMS
RED MOON
BIG MOON

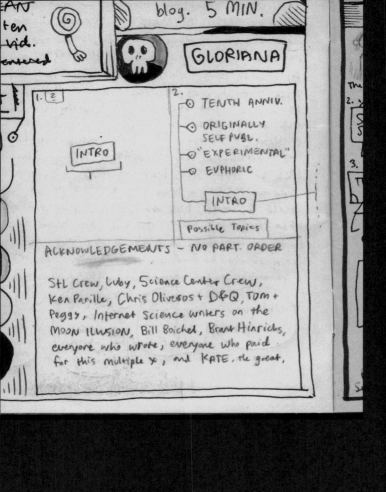

blog. 5 MIN.

AN
ten
vid.
entered

GLORIANA

1. [2]

2.

⊙ TENTH ANNIV.

⊙ ORIGINALLY
   SELF PUBL.

INTRO

⊙ "EXPERIMENTAL"

⊙ EUPHORIC

INTRO

Possible Topics

ACKNOWLEDGEMENTS — NO PART. ORDER

StL Crew, Luby, Science Center Crew,
Ken Parille, Chris Oliveros + D&Q, Tom +
Peggy, Internet Science writers on the
MOON ILLUSION, Bill Boichel, Brant Hinrichs,
everyone who wrote, everyone who paid
for this multiple X, and KATE, the great.

The
2.
S
S

3.

S

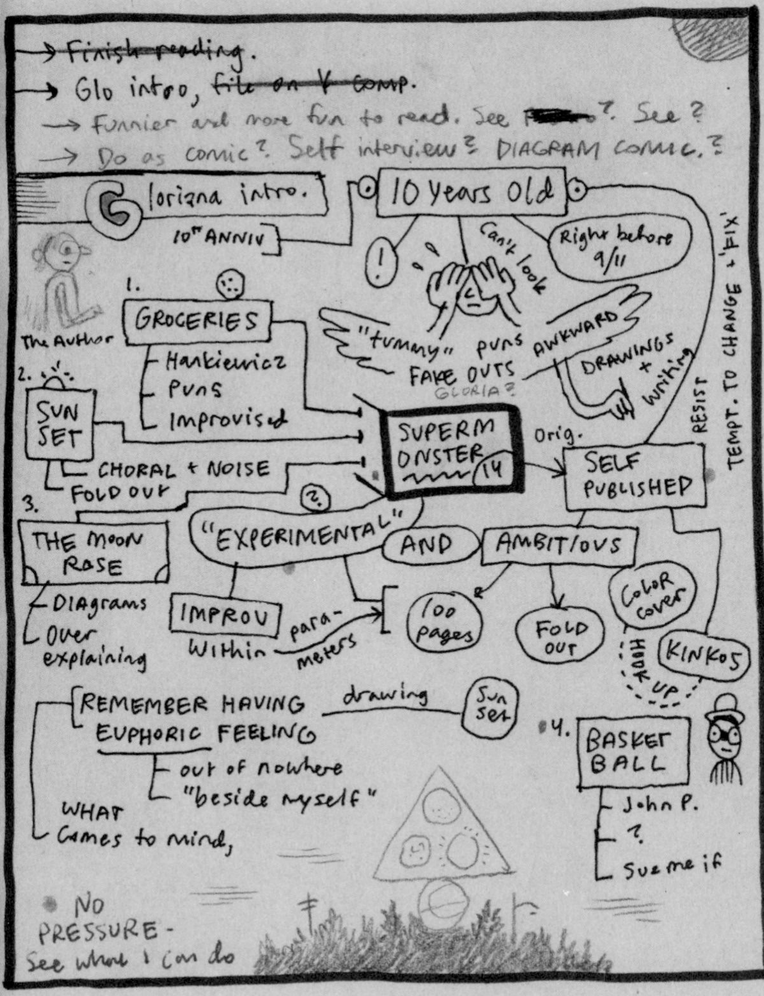

→ Finish reading.
→ Glo intro, file on V comp.
→ Funnier and more fun to read. See [redacted]?. See?
→ Do as comic?. Self interview? DIAGRAM comic.?
Glorianna intro.
10th ANNIV
10 Years Old
!
Can't look
Right before 9/11
The Author
1.
GROCERIES
Hankiewicz
Puns
Improvised
"tummy" puns
FAKE OUTS
GLORIA?
AWKWARD
DRAWINGS + writing
TEMPT. TO CHANGE + 'FIX'
RESIST
2.
SUN SET
SUPERMONSTER 14
Orig.
SELF PUBLISHED
CHORAL + NOISE
FOLD OUT
3.
THE MOON ROSE
Diagrams
Over explaining
"EXPERIMENTAL"
AND
AMBITIOUS
IMPROV
Within parameters
100 pages
FOLD OUT
COLOR COVER
HOOK UP
KINKOS
REMEMBER HAVING EUPHORIC FEELING
drawing
Sun set
out of nowhere
"beside myself"
WHAT comes to mind,
4.
BASKET BALL
John P.
?
Sue me if
NO PRESSURE -
See what I can do

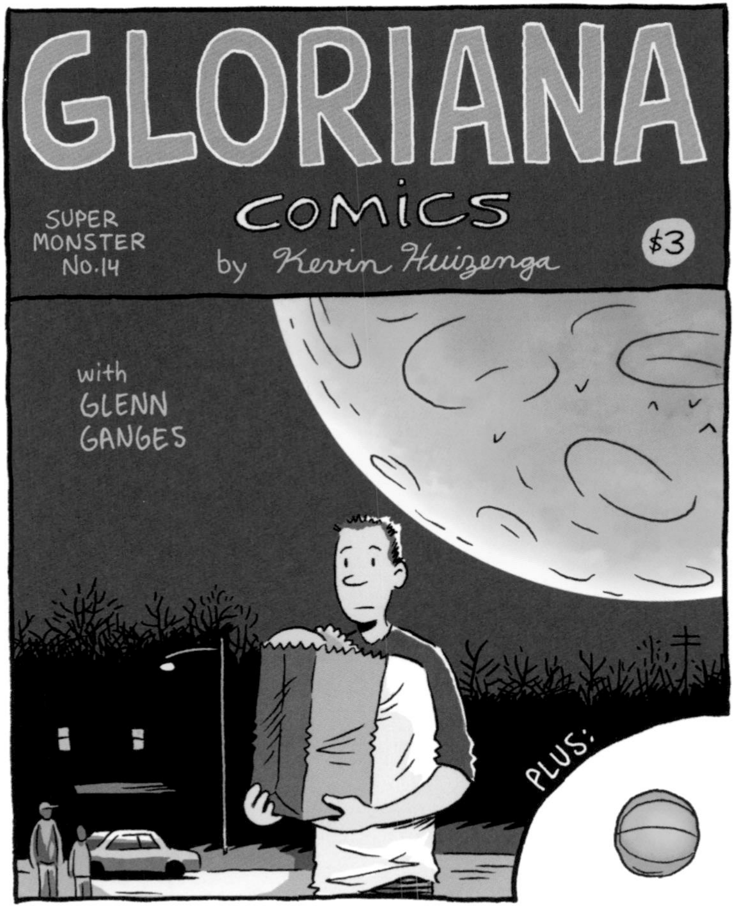
GLORIANA
COMICS
SUPER MONSTER No.14
by Kevin Huizenga
$3
with GLENN GANGES
PLUS:

Cover, Supermonster #14 (2001)

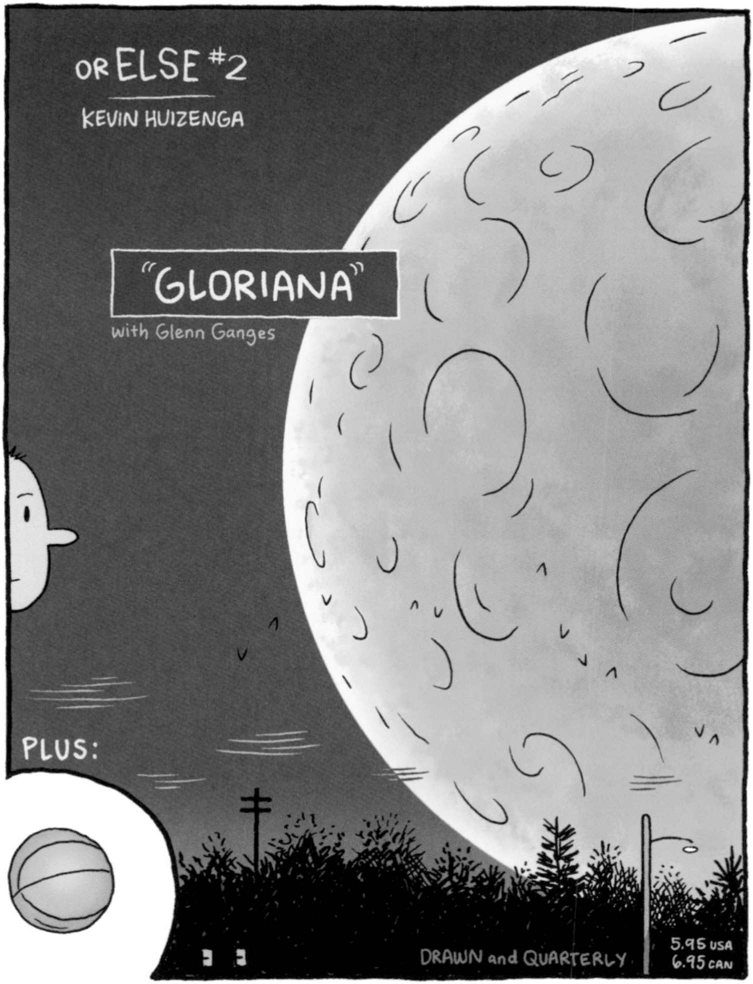
OR ELSE #2
KEVIN HUIZENGA
"GLORIANA"
with Glenn Ganges
PLUS:
DRAWN and QUARTERLY
5.95 USA
6.95 CAN

Cover, Or Else #2 (2004)

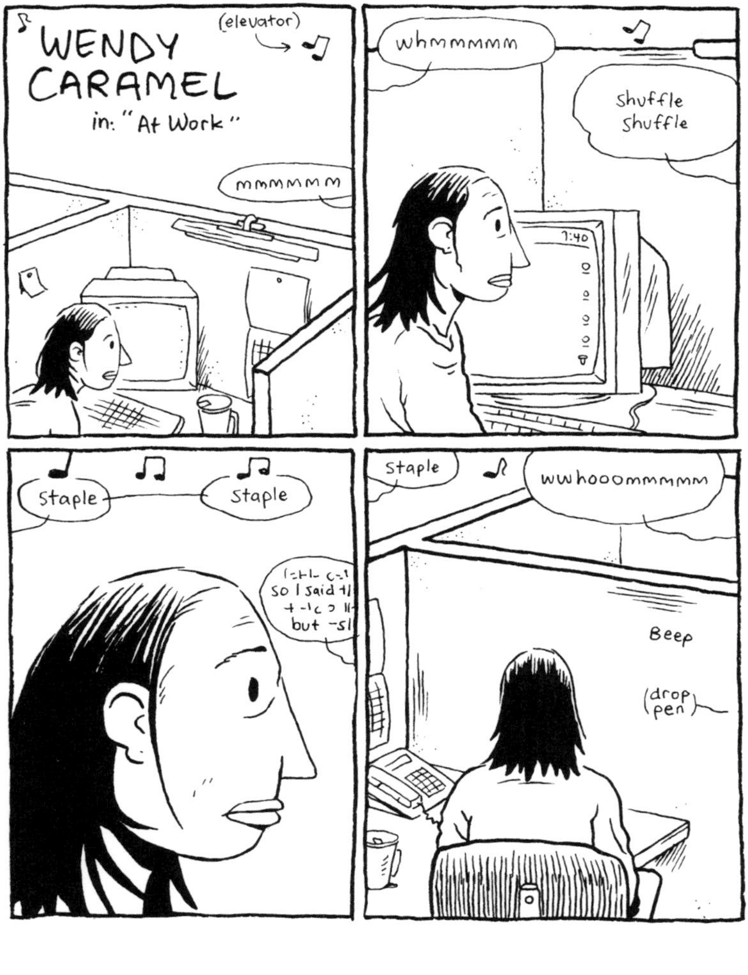
WENDY CARAMEL
in: "At Work"
(elevator)
mmmmmm
whmmmmm
shuffle shuffle
1:40
staple
staple
so I said
but
staple
wwhooommmmm
Beep
(drop pen)

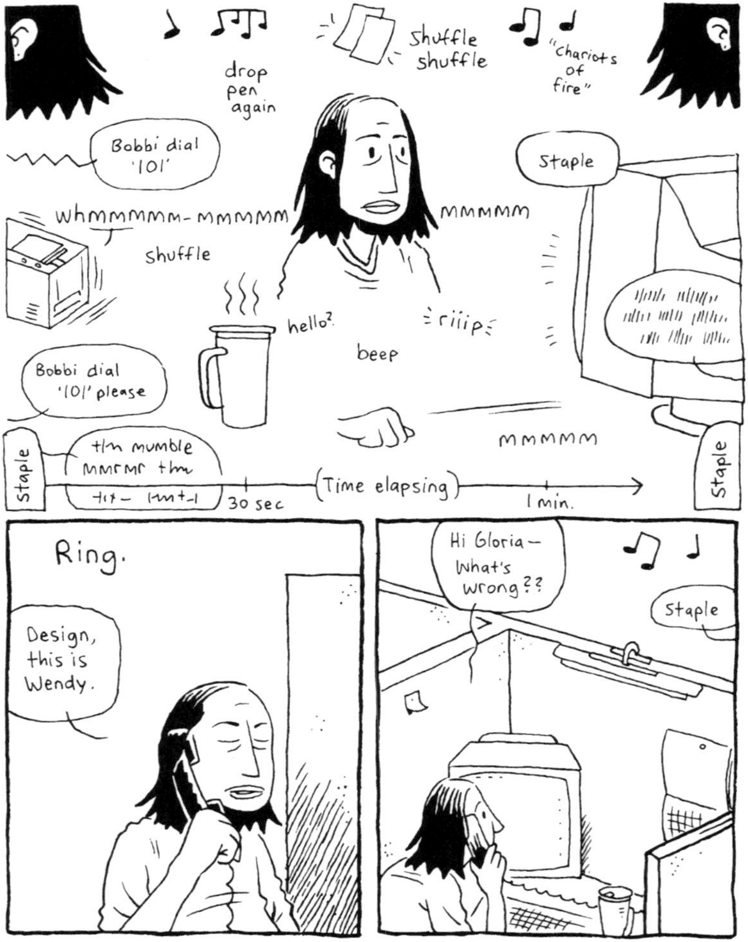

drop pen again
shuffle shuffle
"chariots of fire"
Bobbi dial '101'
Staple
whmmmmm-mmmmm
mmmmm
shuffle
hello?
riiip
beep
Bobbi dial '101' please
Staple
mmmmm
Staple
30 sec
(Time elapsing)
1 min.
Ring.
Design, this is Wendy.
Hi Gloria - What's wrong??
Staple

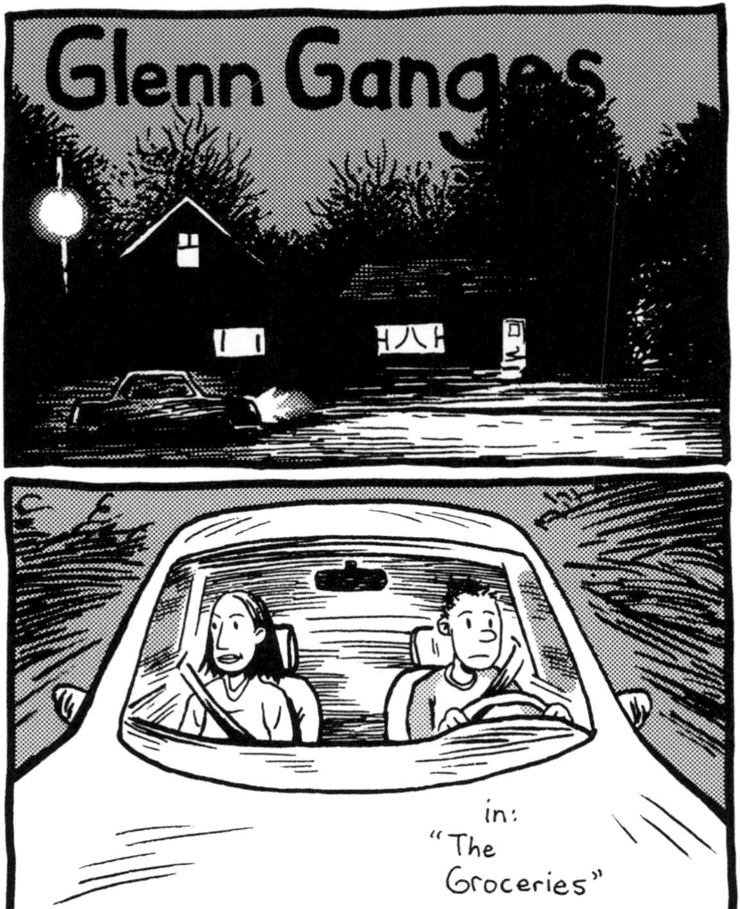
Glenn Ganges
in:
"The
Groceries"

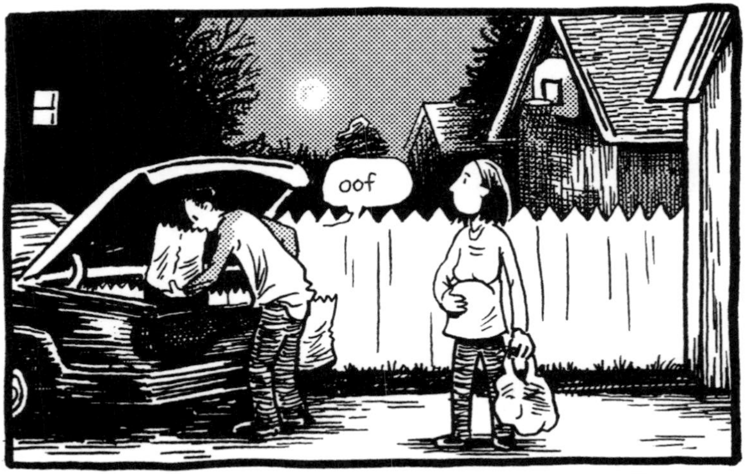
oof

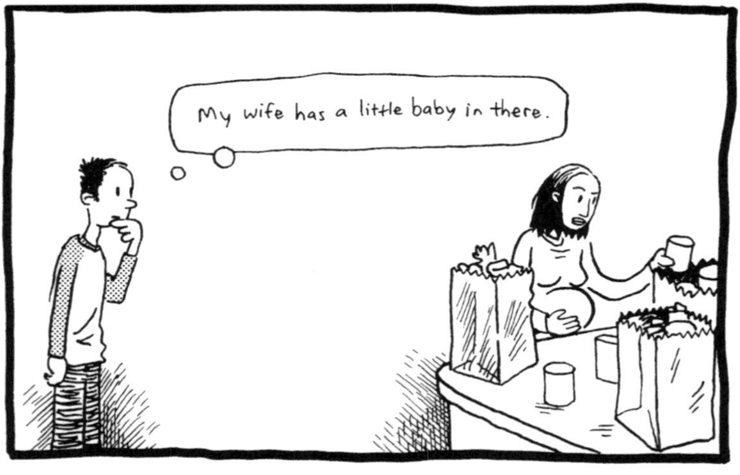
My wife has a little baby in there.

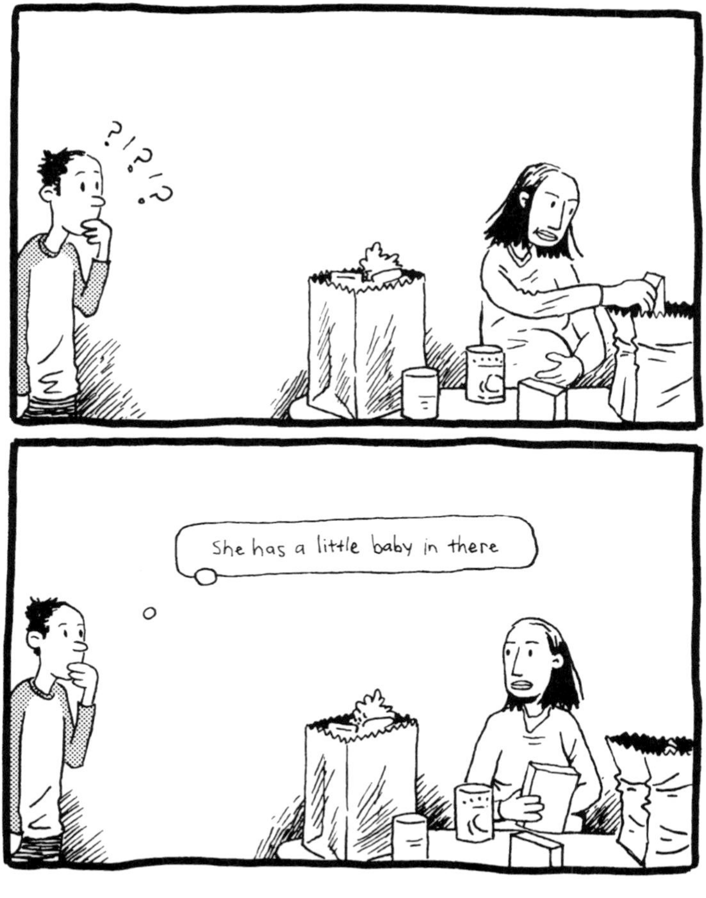
?!?!?
She has a little baby in there

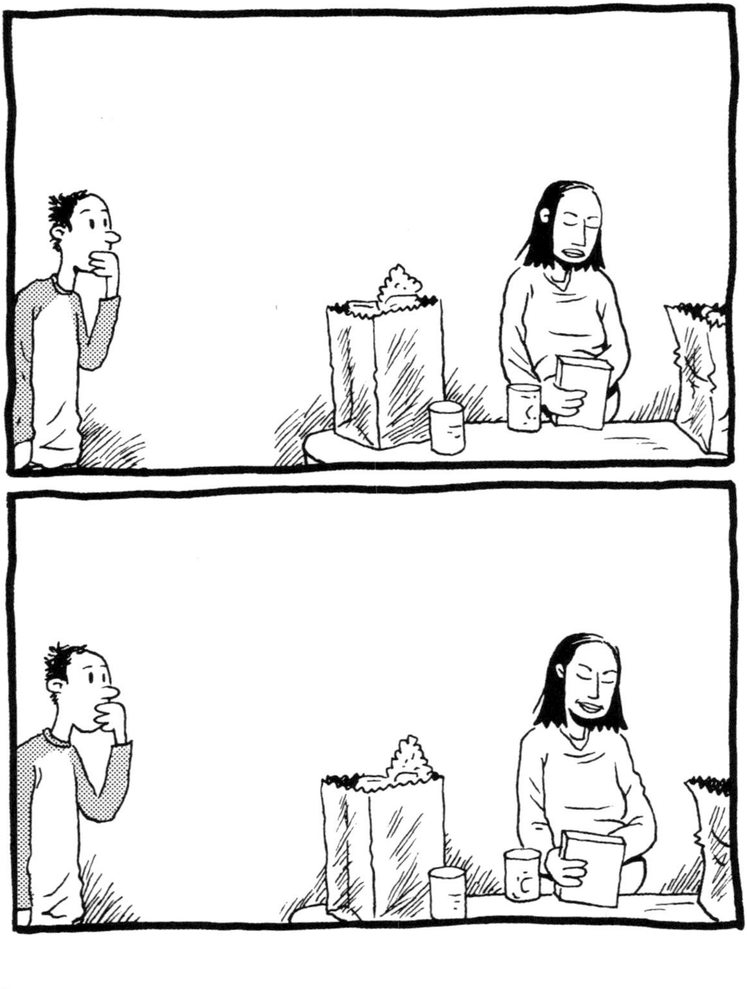

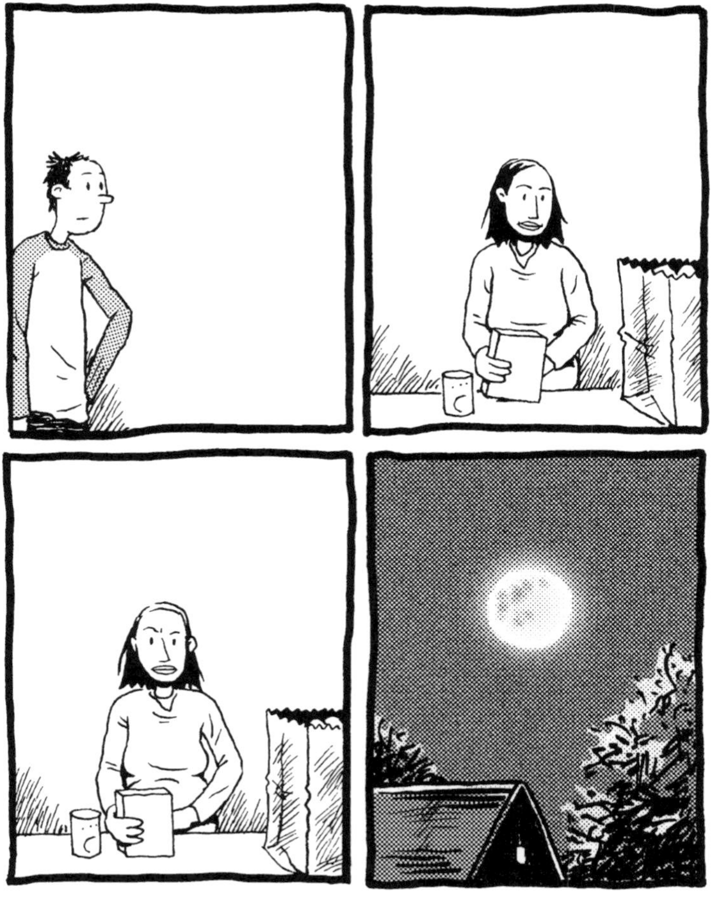

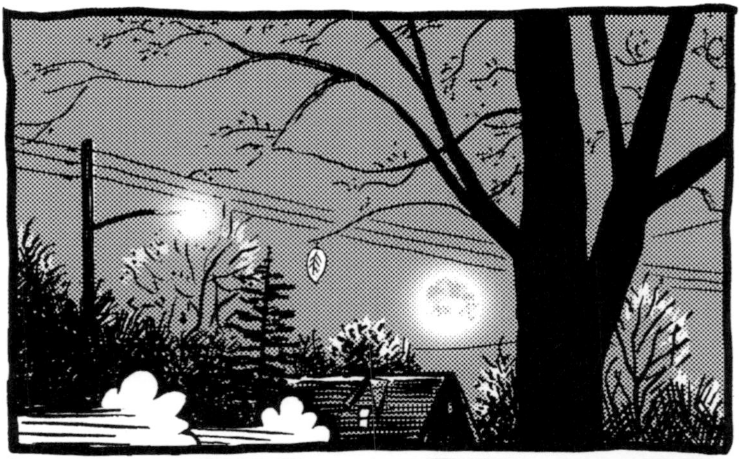

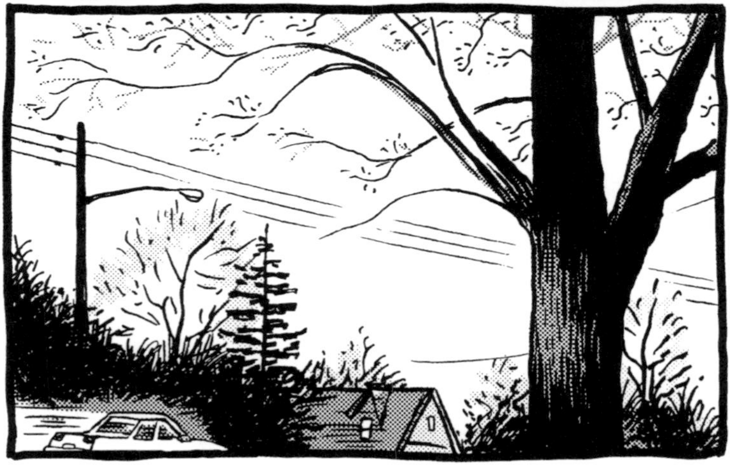

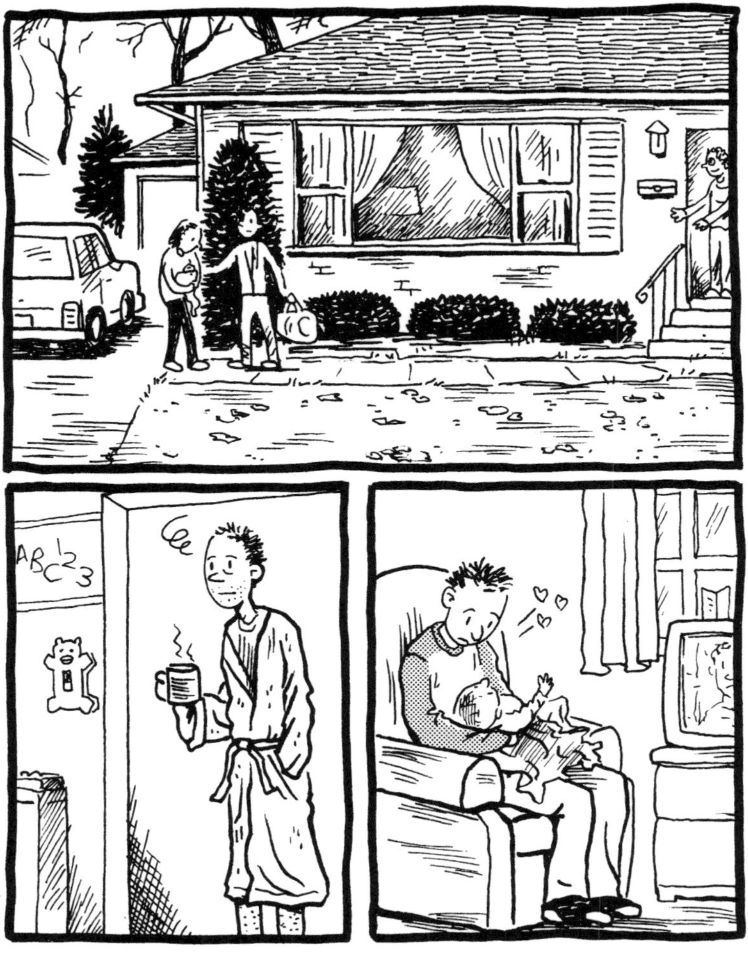
ABC123

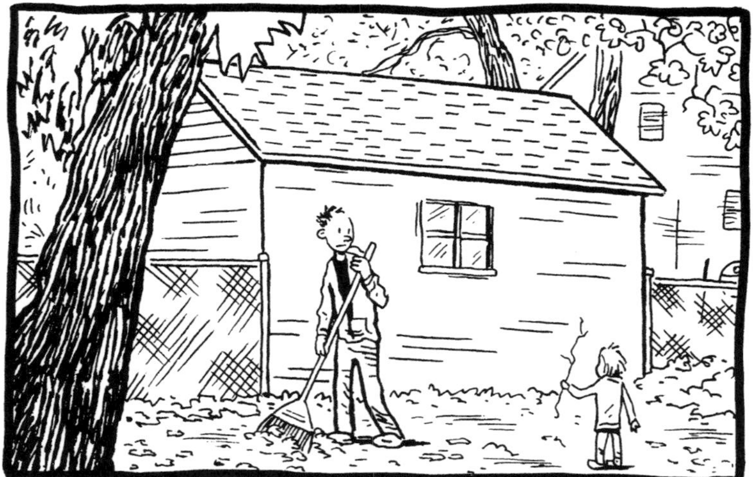

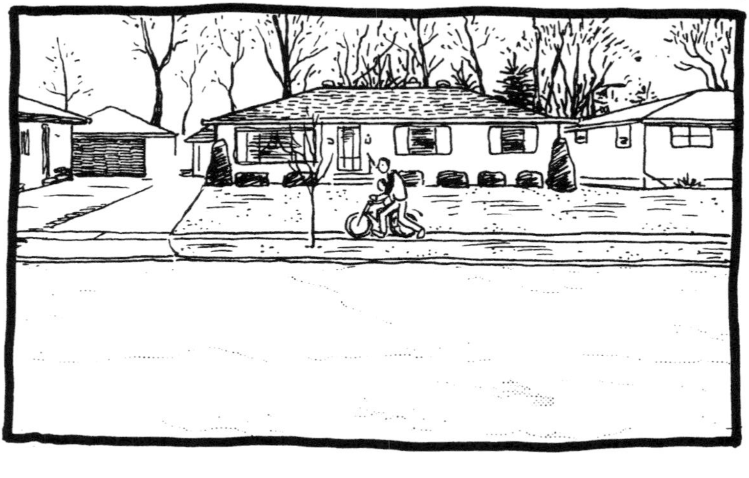

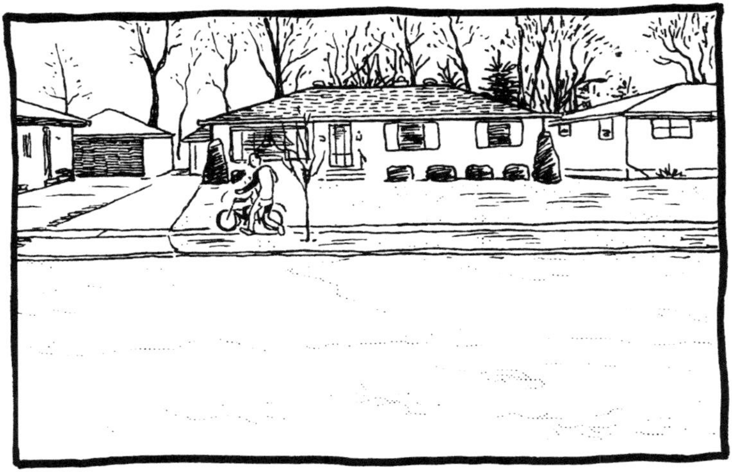

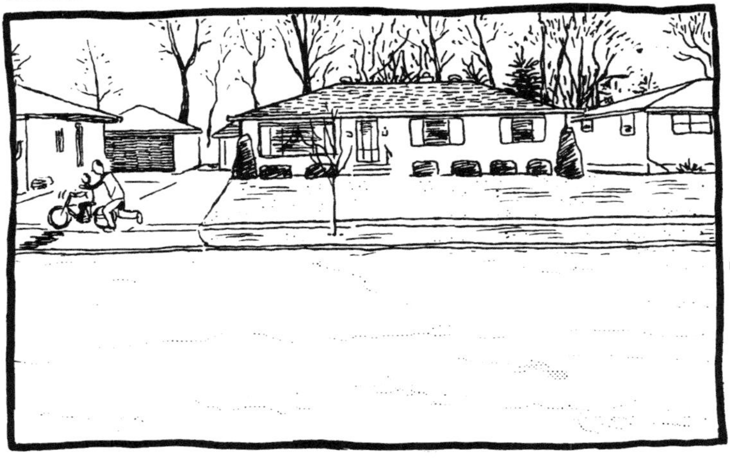

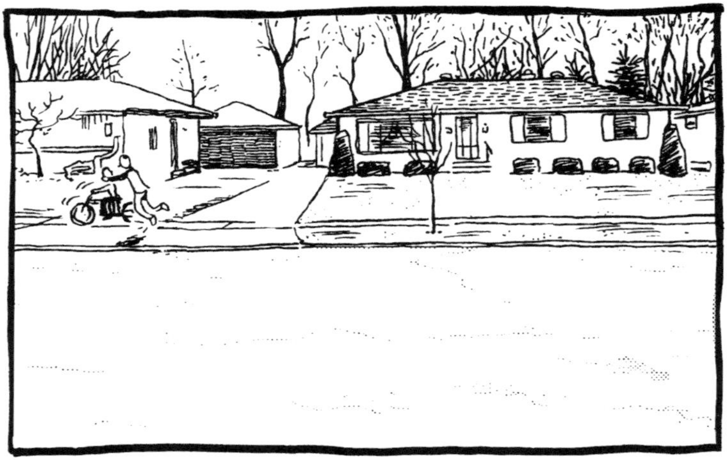

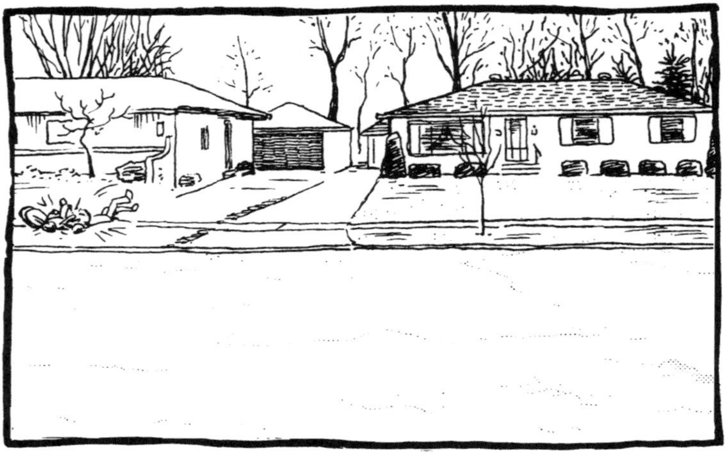

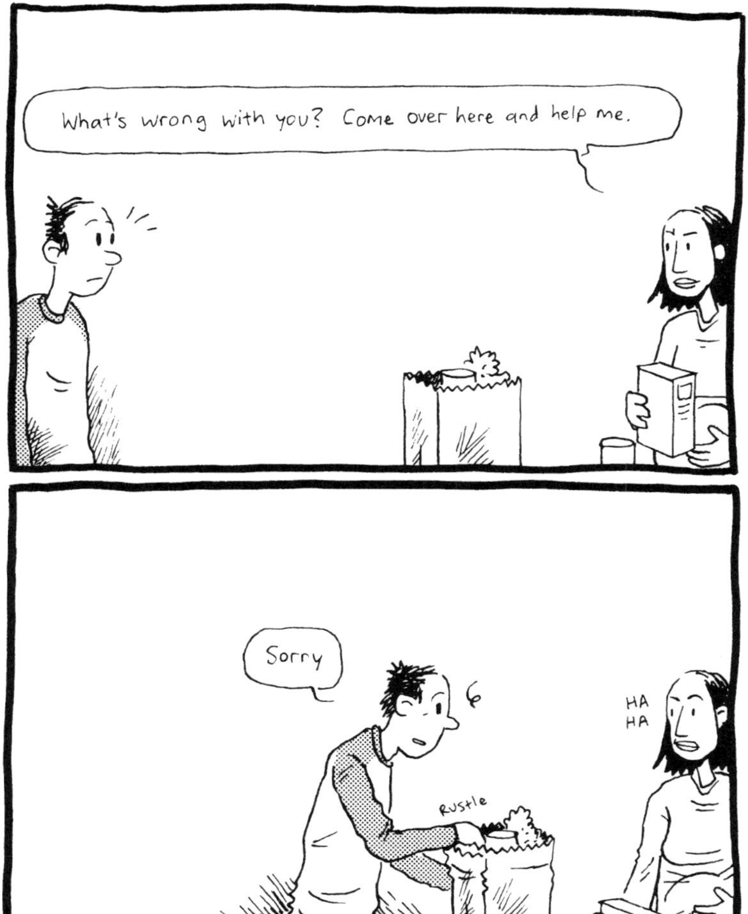
What's wrong with you? Come over here and help me.
Sorry
Rustle
HA HA

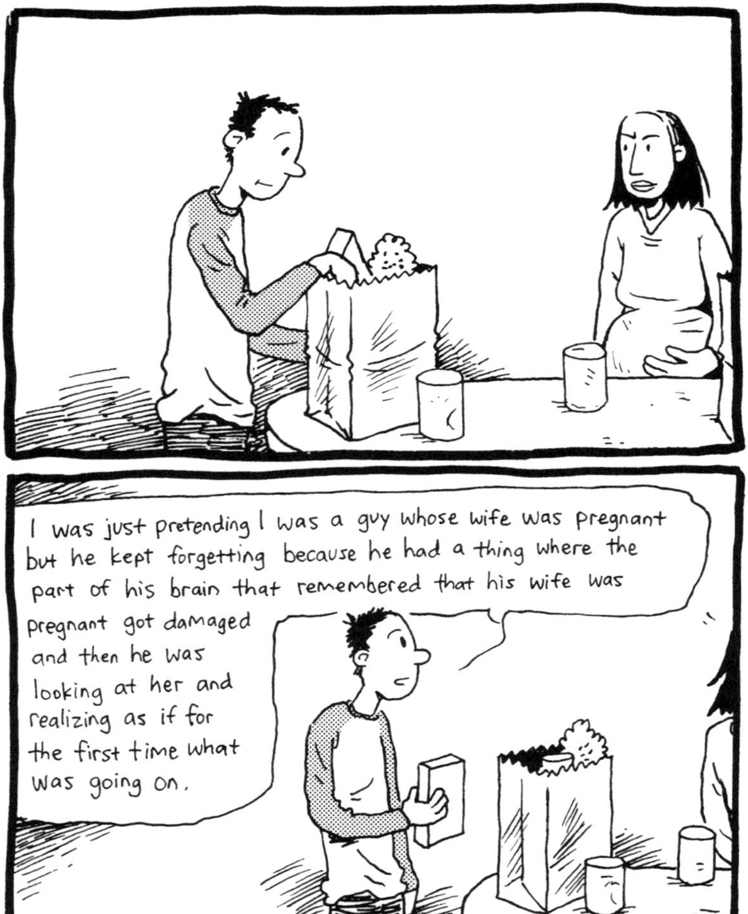
I was just pretending I was a guy whose wife was pregnant but he kept forgetting because he had a thing where the part of his brain that remembered that his wife was pregnant got damaged and then he was looking at her and realizing as if for the first time what was going on.

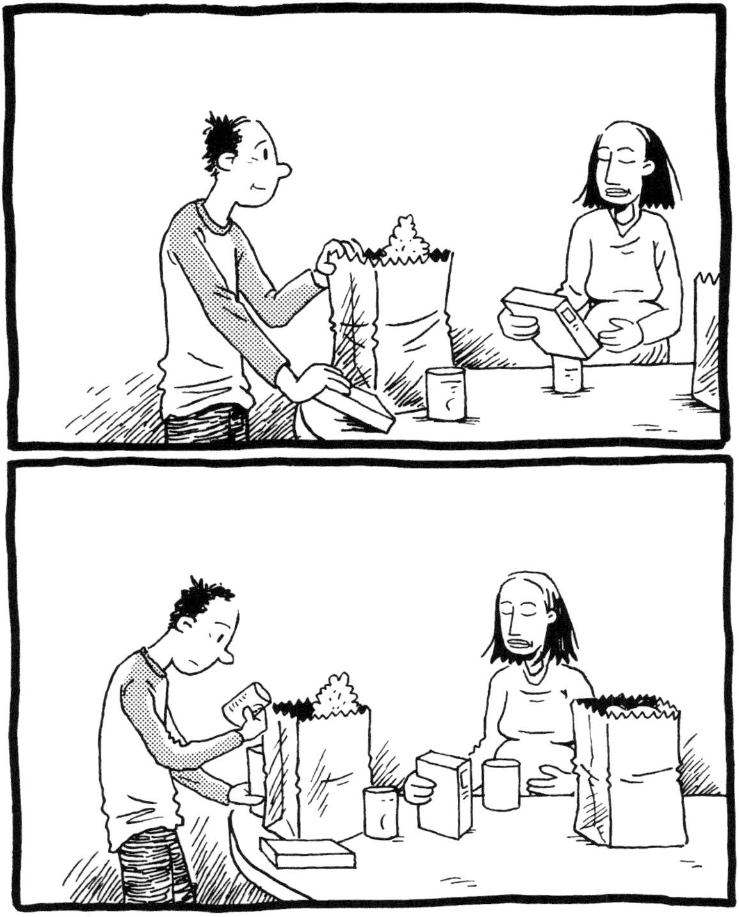

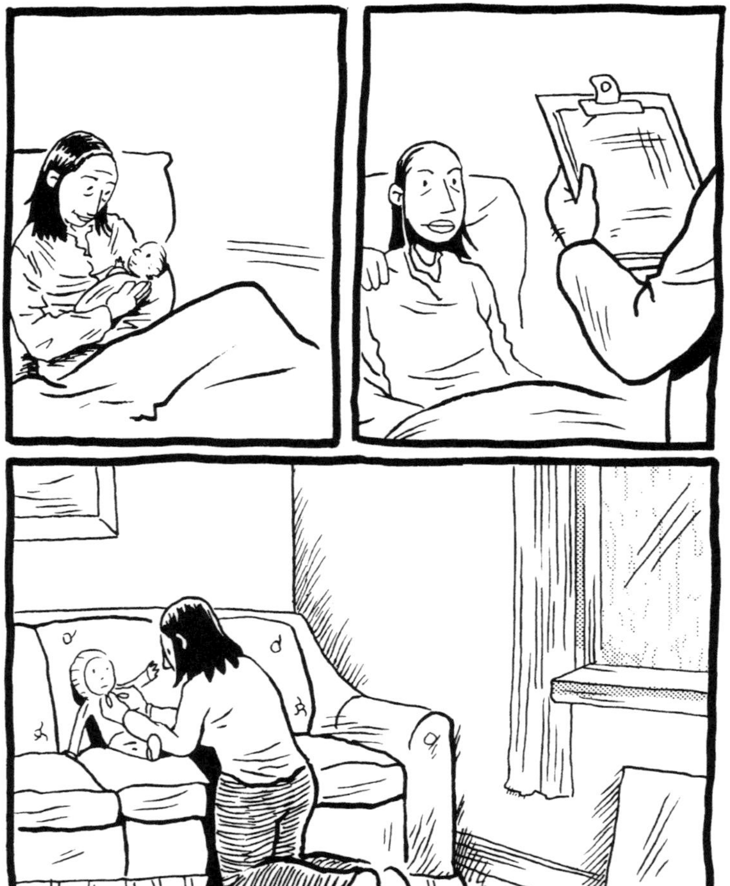

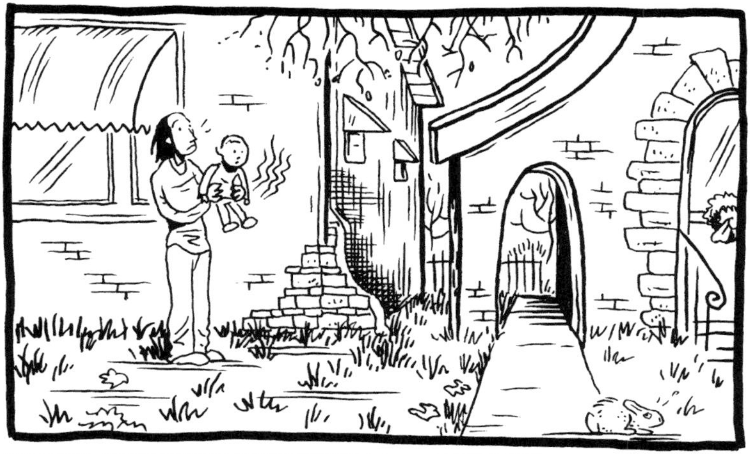

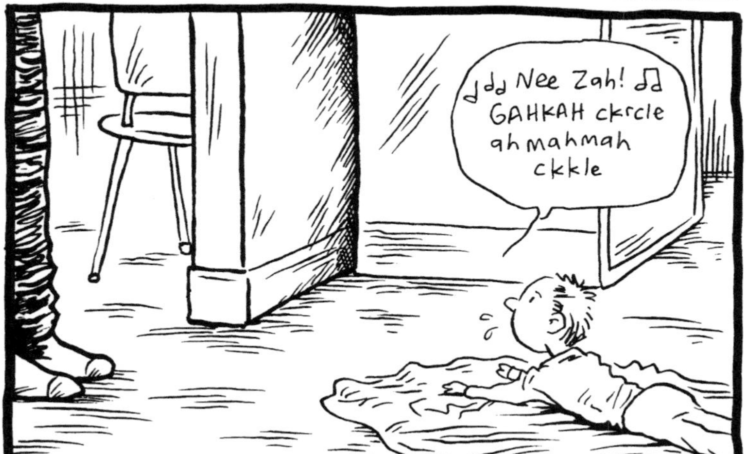
♩♫ Nee Zah! ♫ GAHKAH ckrcle ahmahmah ckkle

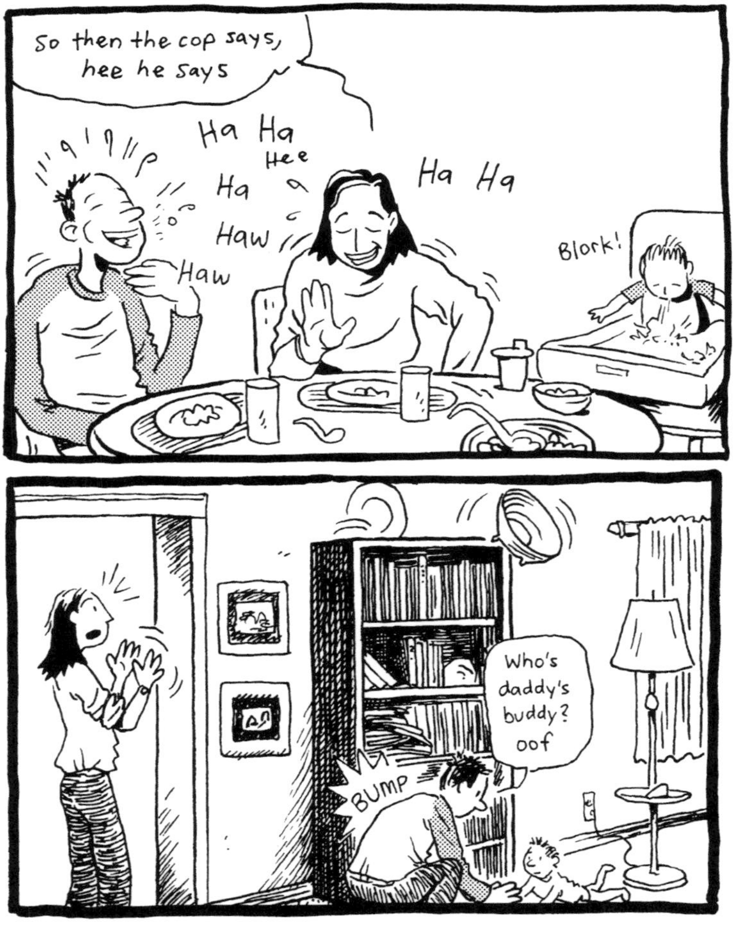

So then the cop says, hee he says
Ha Ha
Hee
Ha
Haw
Haw
Ha Ha
Blork!
Who's daddy's buddy? oof
BUMP

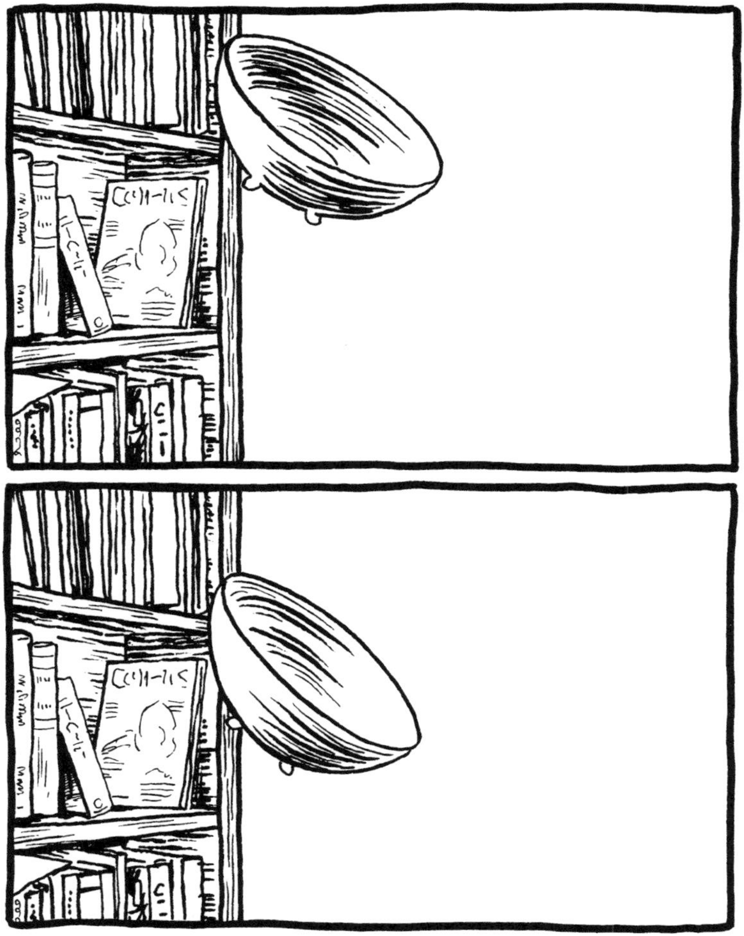

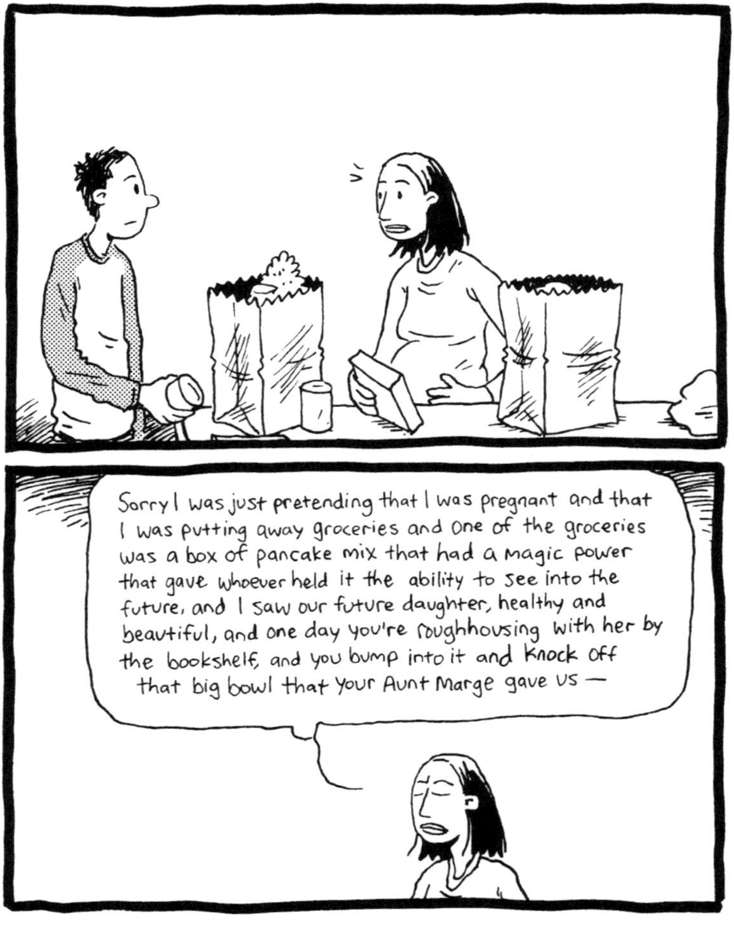
Sorry I was just pretending that I was pregnant and that I was putting away groceries and one of the groceries was a box of pancake mix that had a magic power that gave whoever held it the ability to see into the future, and I saw our future daughter, healthy and beautiful, and one day you're roughhousing with her by the bookshelf, and you bump into it and knock off that big bowl that your Aunt Marge gave us —

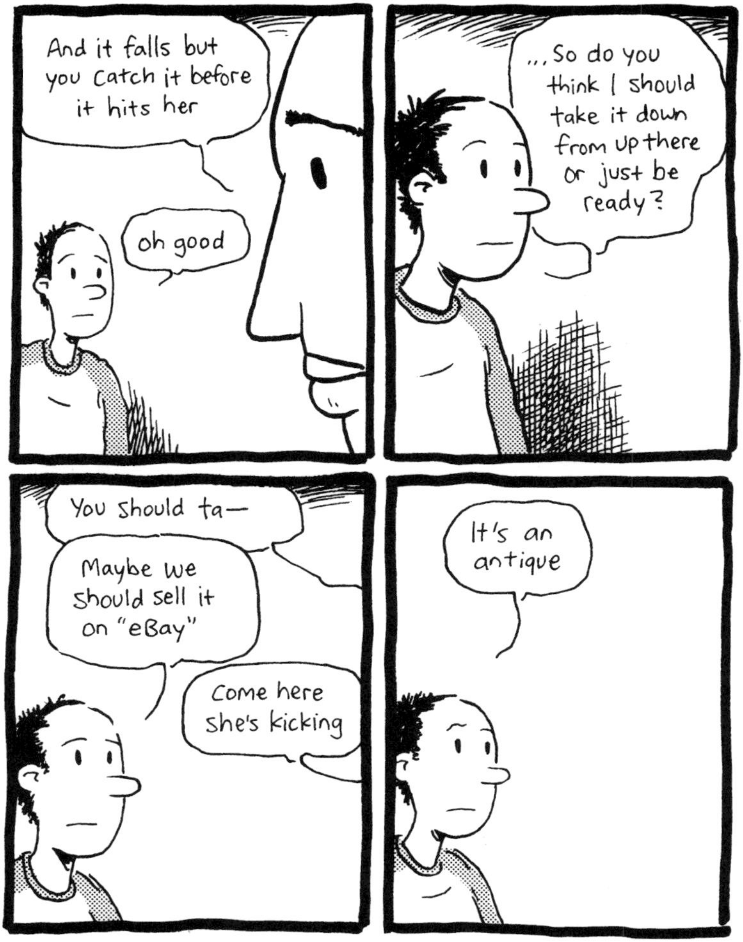
And it falls but you catch it before it hits her
oh good
...So do you think I should take it down from up there or just be ready?
You should ta—
Maybe we should sell it on "eBay"
Come here she's kicking
It's an antique

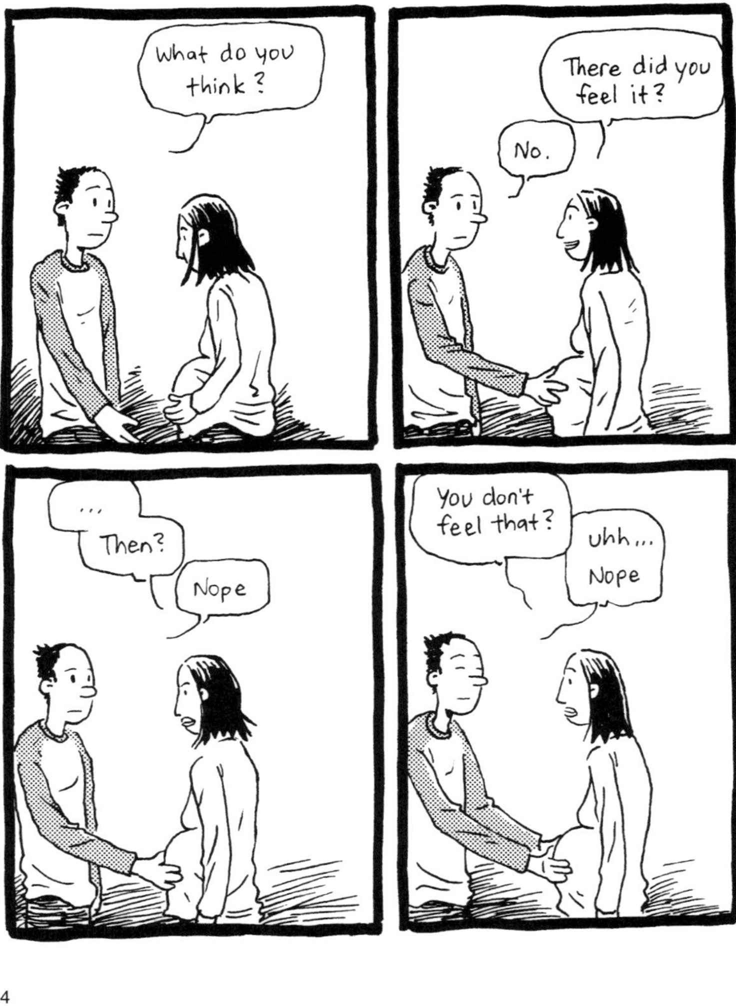
What do you think?
There did you feel it?
No.
...
Then?
Nope
You don't feel that?
uhh...
Nope

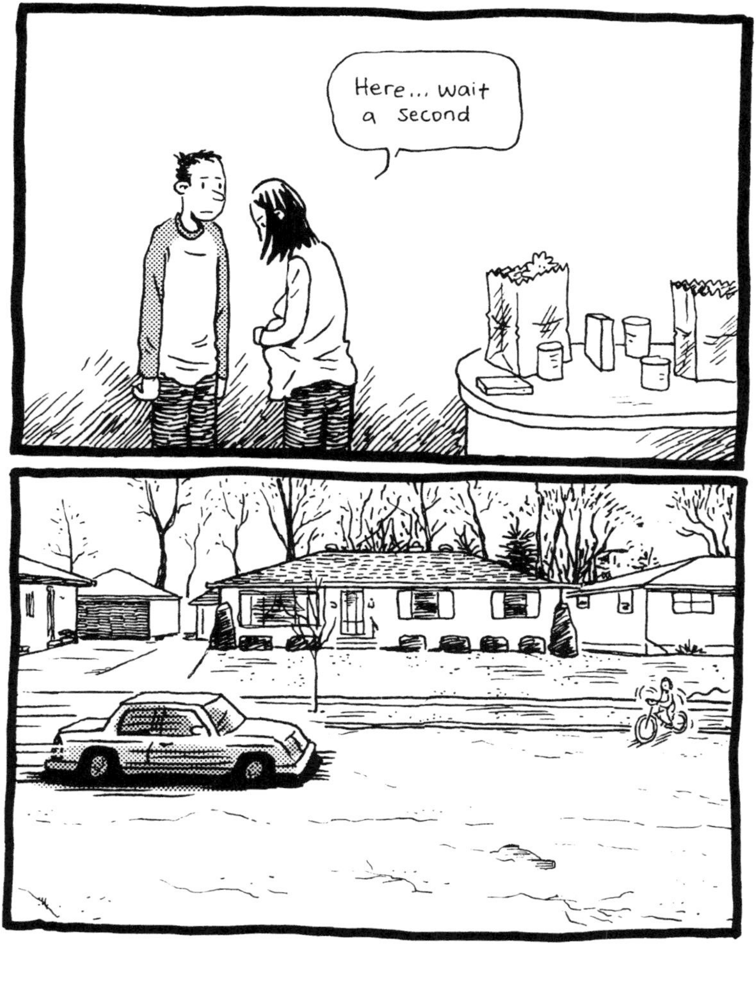
Here... wait a second

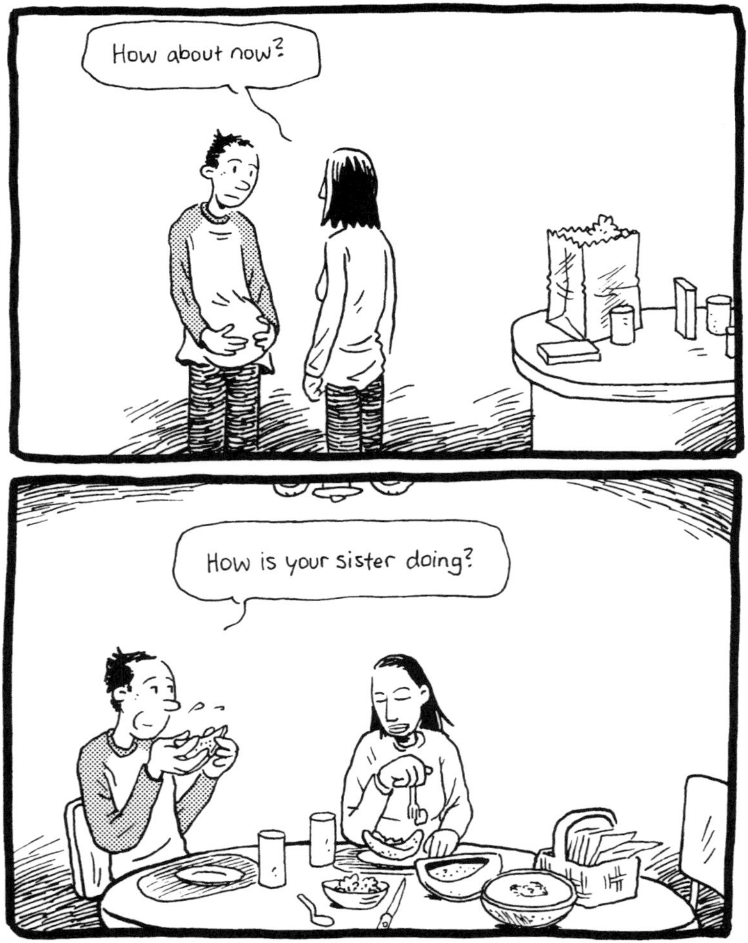
How about now?
How is your sister doing?

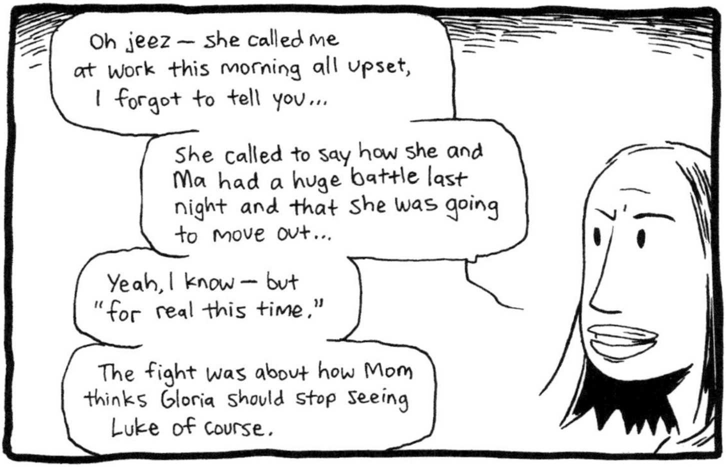
Oh jeez — she called me at work this morning all upset, I forgot to tell you...
She called to say how she and Ma had a huge battle last night and that she was going to move out...
Yeah, I know — but "for real this time."
The fight was about how Mom thinks Gloria should stop seeing Luke of course.

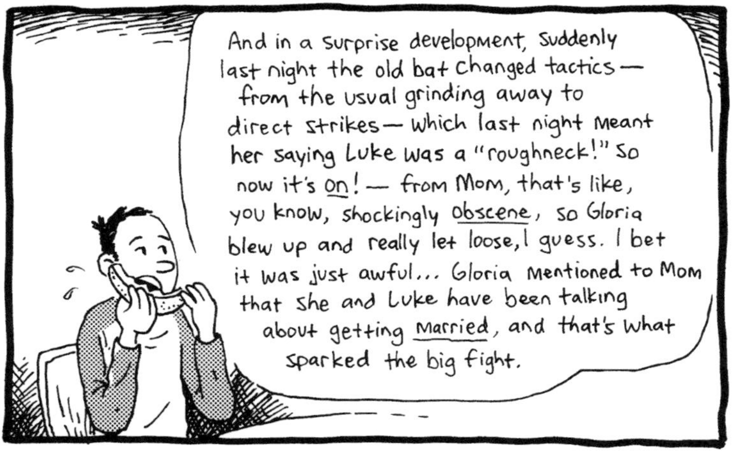
And in a surprise development, suddenly last night the old bat changed tactics — from the usual grinding away to direct strikes — which last night meant her saying Luke was a "roughneck!" So now it's on! — from Mom, that's like, you know, shockingly obscene, so Gloria blew up and really let loose, I guess. I bet it was just awful... Gloria mentioned to Mom that she and Luke have been talking about getting married, and that's what sparked the big fight.

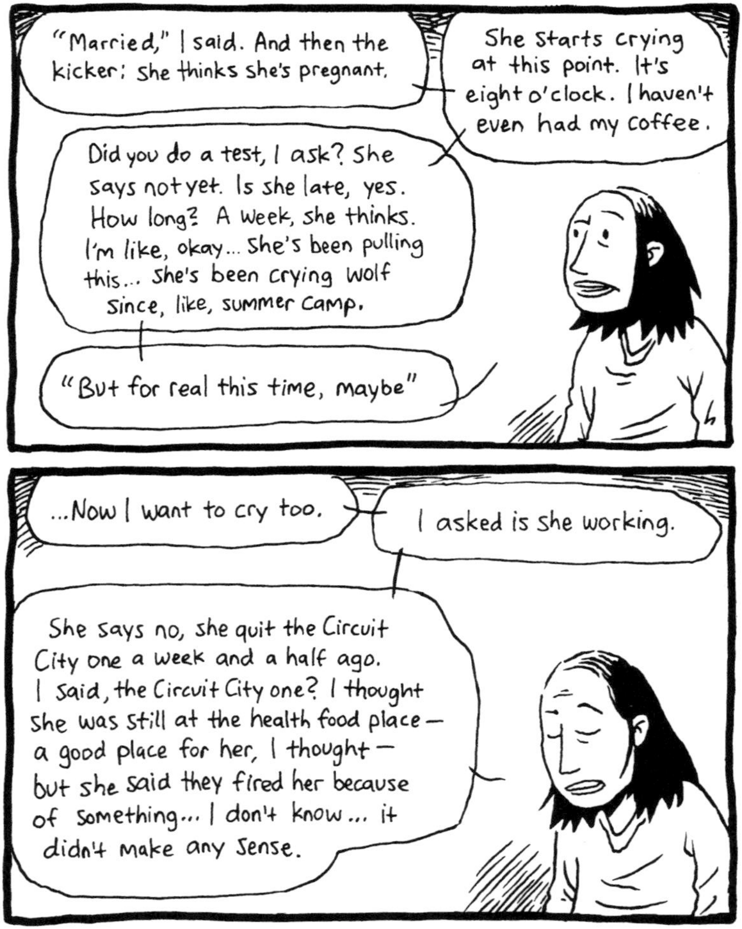
"Married," I said. And then the kicker: she thinks she's pregnant.
She starts crying at this point. It's eight o'clock. I haven't even had my coffee.
Did you do a test, I ask? She says not yet. Is she late, yes. How long? A week, she thinks. I'm like, okay... She's been pulling this... she's been crying wolf since, like, summer camp.
"But for real this time, maybe"
...Now I want to cry too.
I asked is she working.
She says no, she quit the Circuit City one a week and a half ago. I said, the Circuit City one? I thought she was still at the health food place – a good place for her, I thought – but she said they fired her because of something... I don't know... it didn't make any sense.

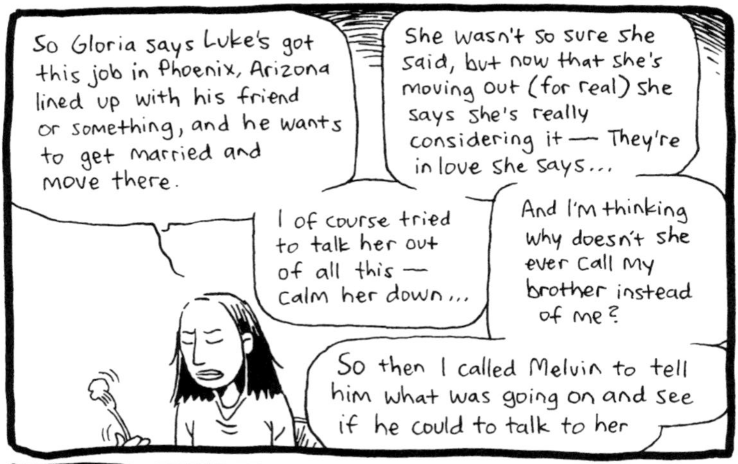
So Gloria says Luke's got this job in Phoenix, Arizona lined up with his friend or something, and he wants to get married and move there.
She wasn't so sure she said, but now that she's moving out (for real) she says she's really considering it — They're in love she says...
I of course tried to talk her out of all this — calm her down...
And I'm thinking why doesn't she ever call my brother instead of me?
So then I called Melvin to tell him what was going on and see if he could to talk to her

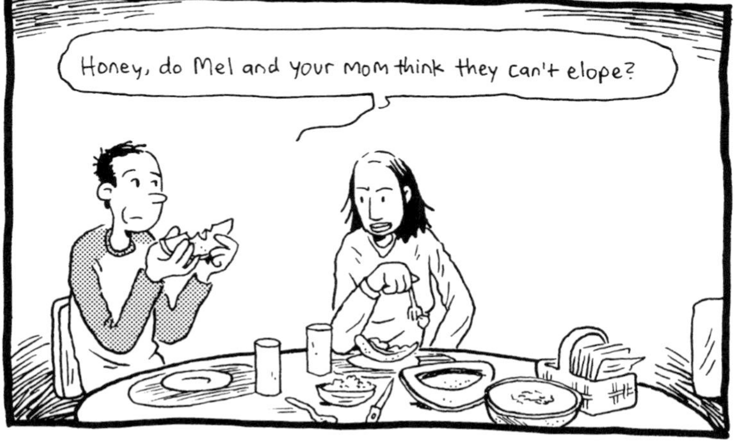
Honey, do Mel and your mom think they can't elope?

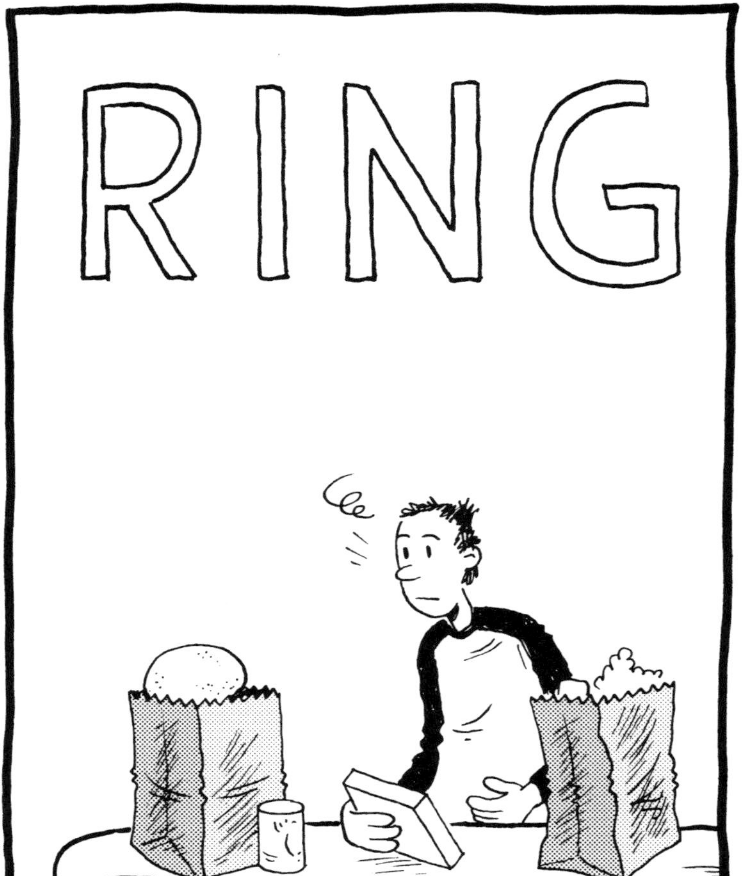
RING

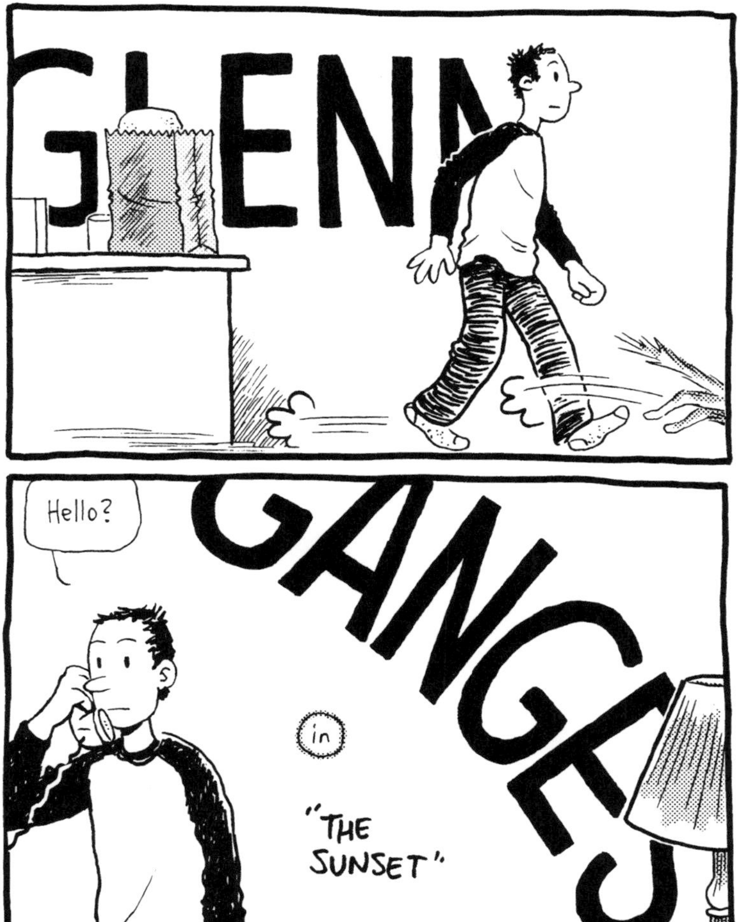
GLENN
Hello?
GANGES
in
"THE SUNSET"

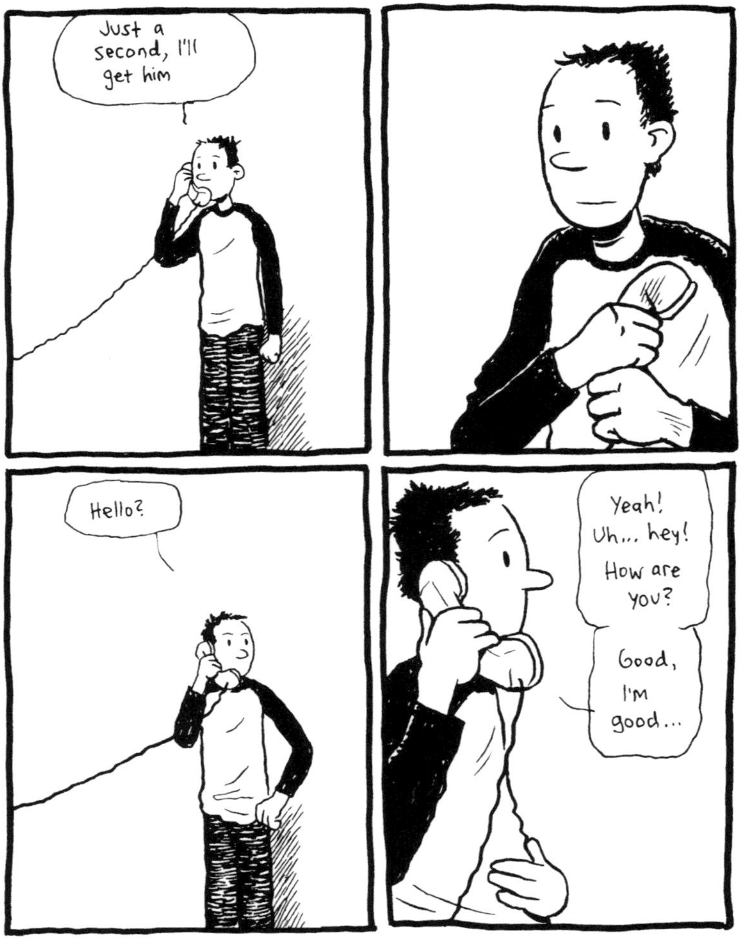
Just a second, I'll get him
Hello?
Yeah! Uh... hey! How are you?
Good, I'm good...

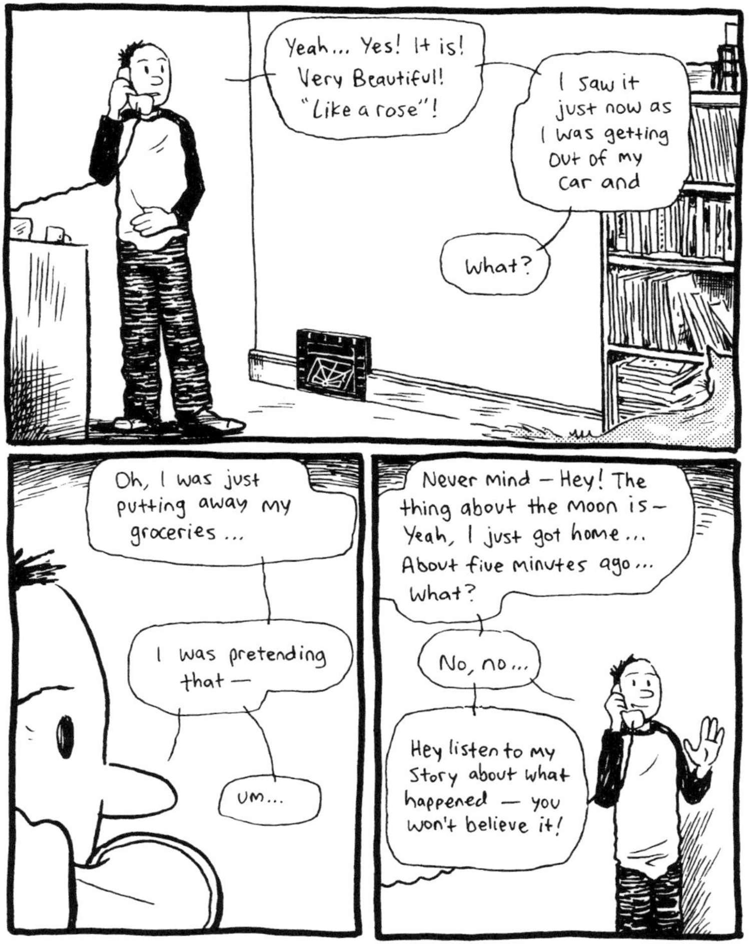
Yeah... Yes! It is! Very Beautiful! "Like a rose"!
I saw it just now as I was getting out of my car and
What?
Oh, I was just putting away my groceries...
I was pretending that —
um...
Never mind — Hey! The thing about the moon is — Yeah, I just got home... About five minutes ago... What?
No, no...
Hey listen to my story about what happened — you won't believe it!

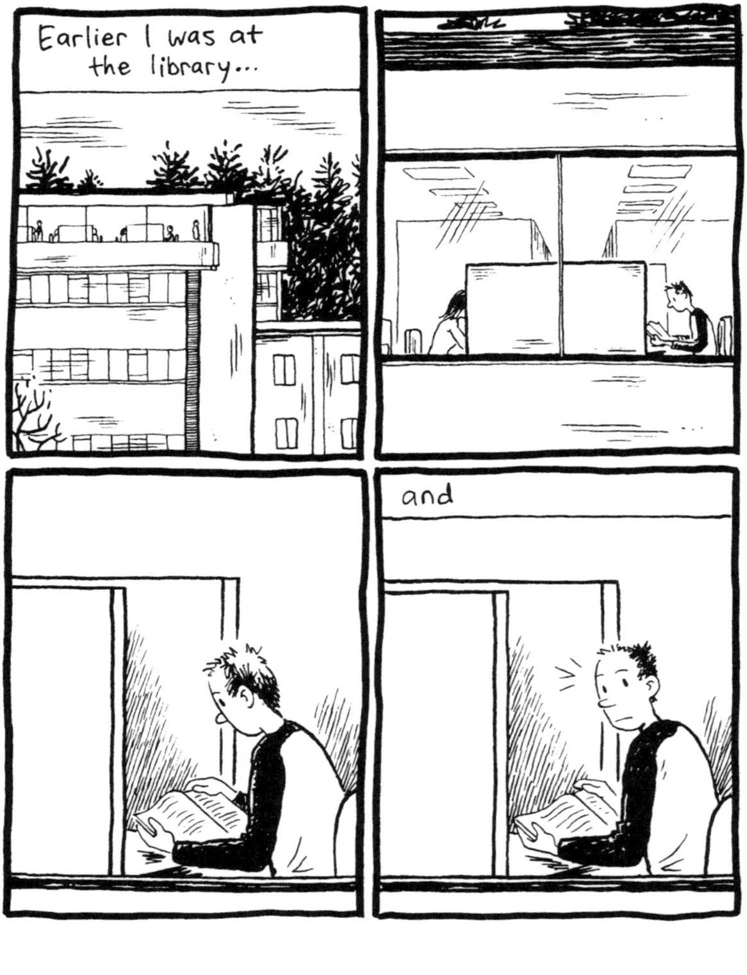
Earlier I was at the library...
and

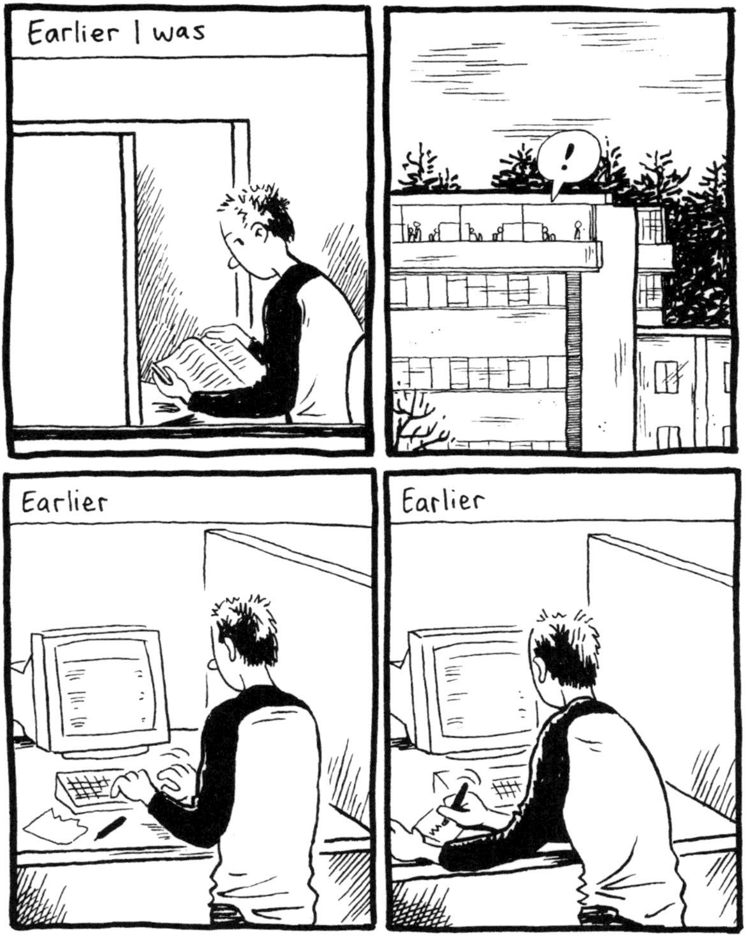
Earlier I was
!
Earlier
Earlier

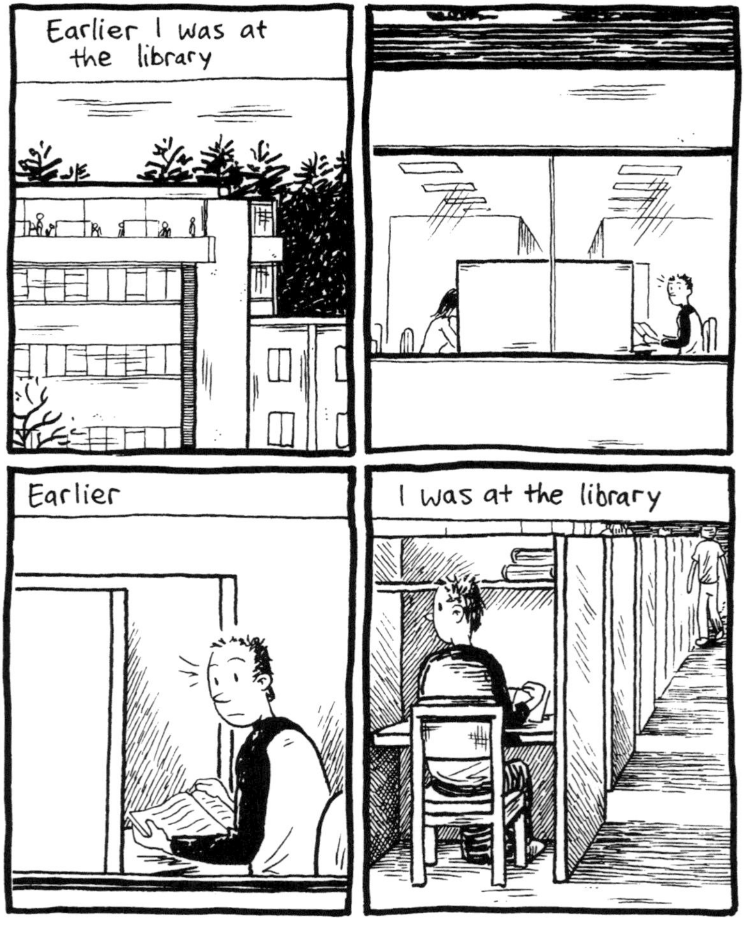
Earlier I was at the library
Earlier
I was at the library

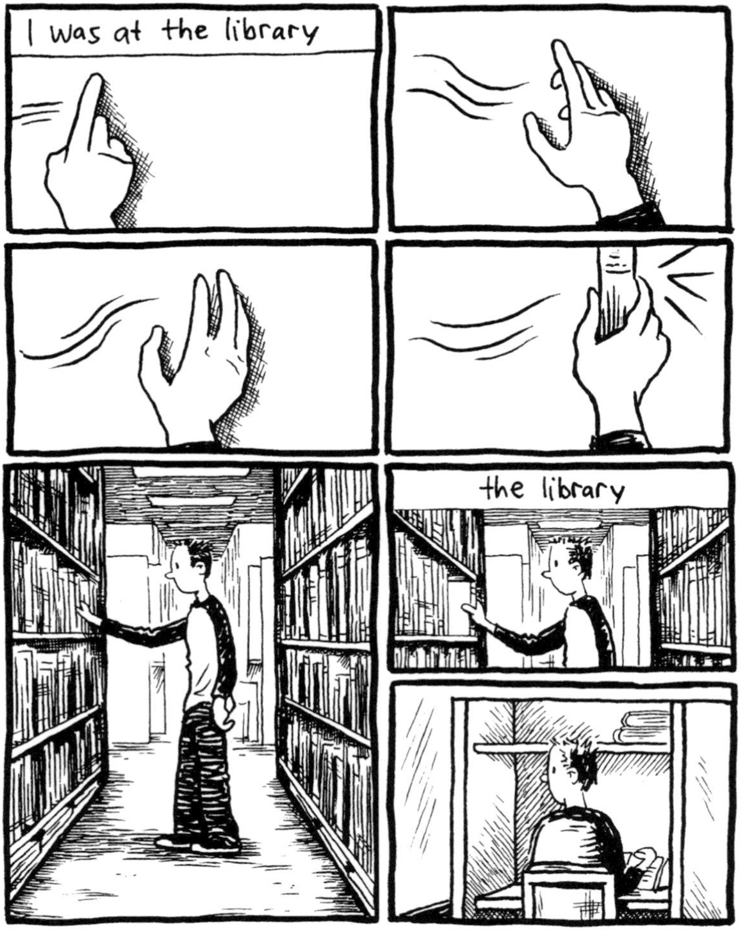
I was at the library
the library

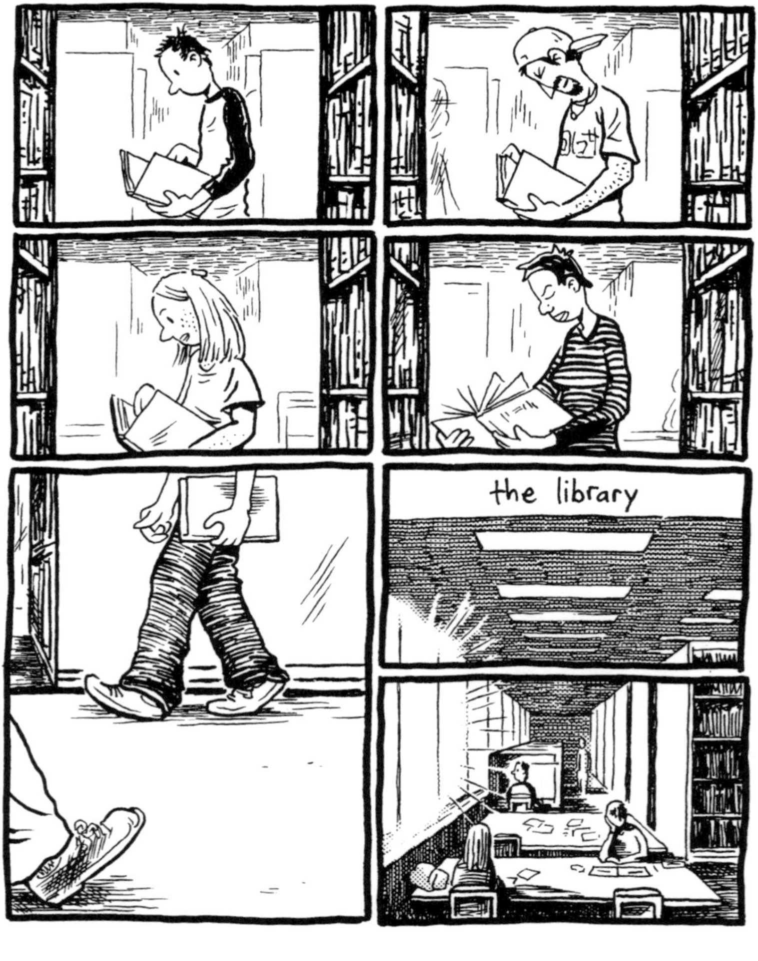
the library

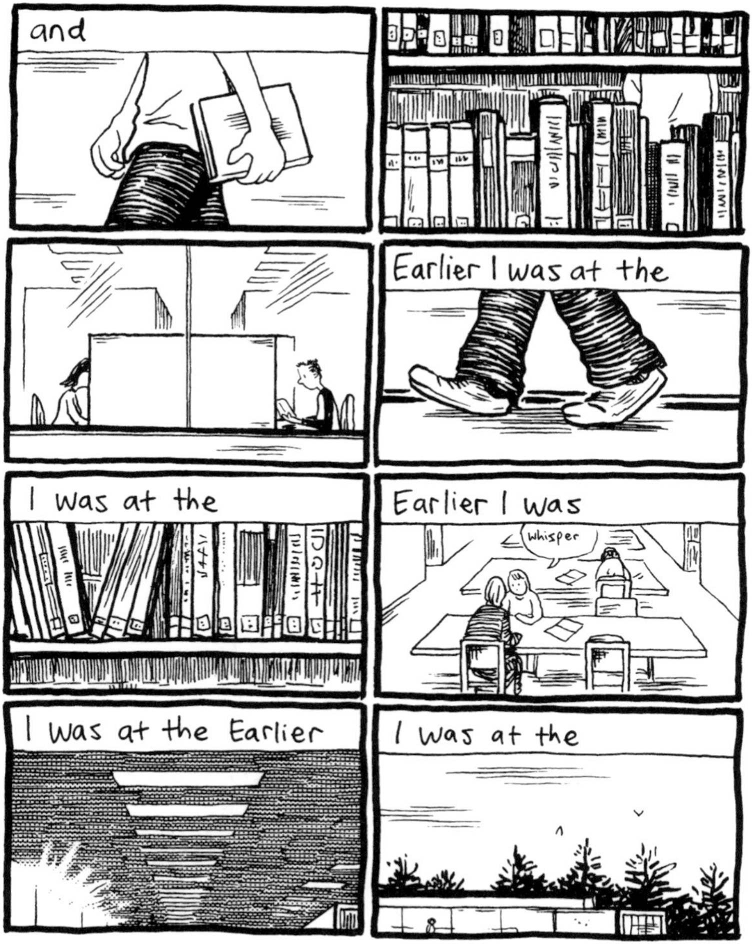
and
Earlier I was at the
I was at the
Earlier I was
whisper
I was at the Earlier
I was at the

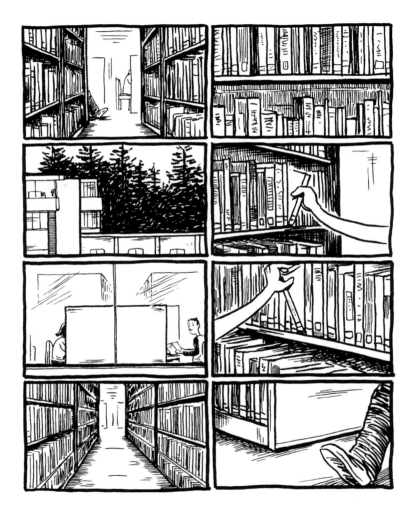

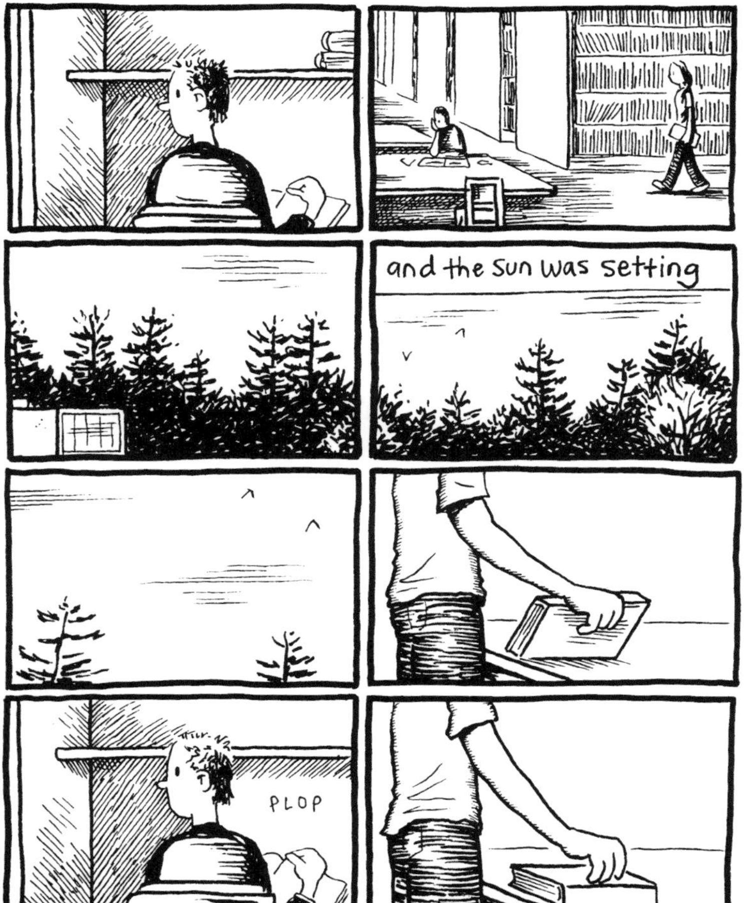
and the sun was setting
PLOP

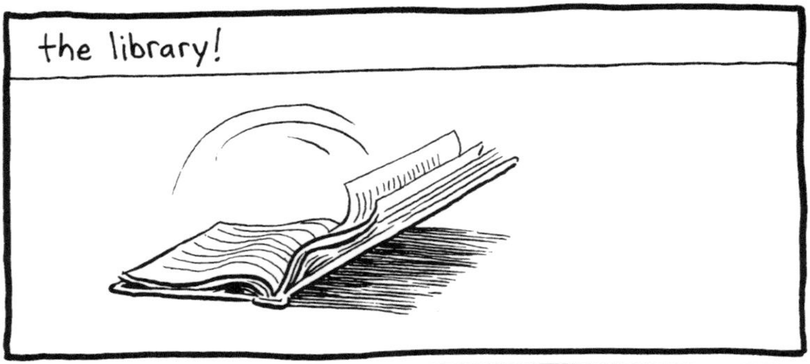
the library!

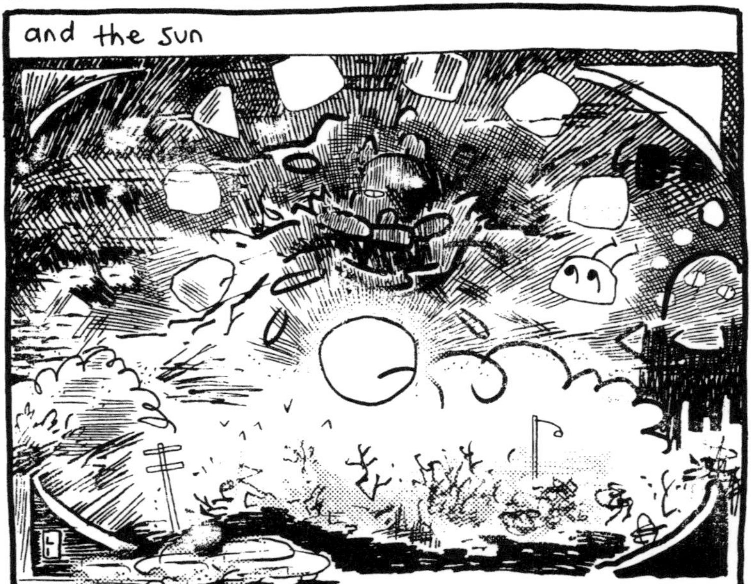
and the sun

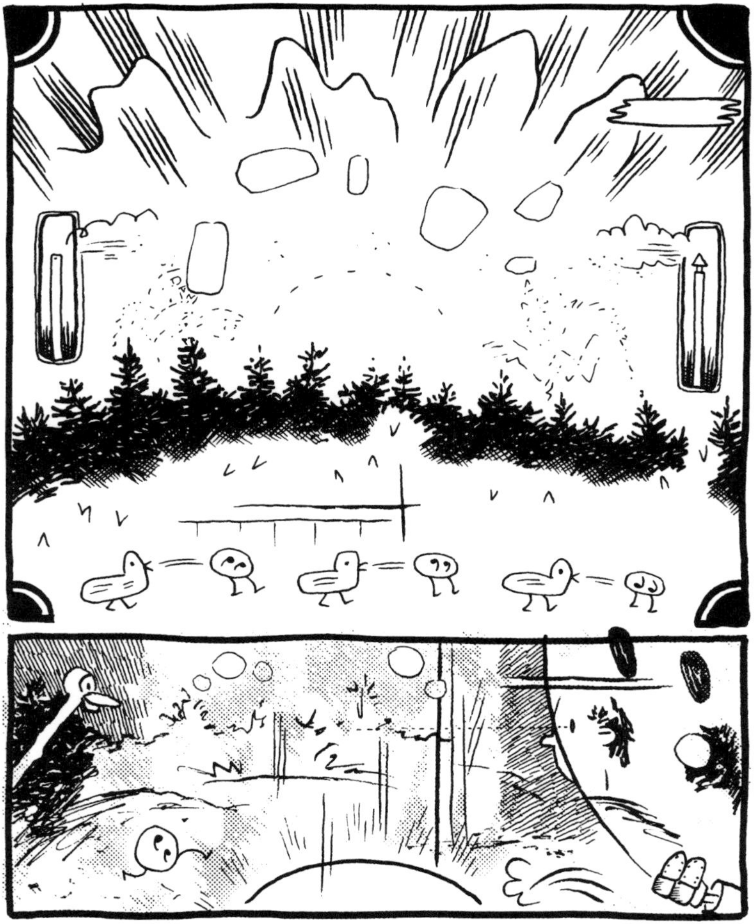

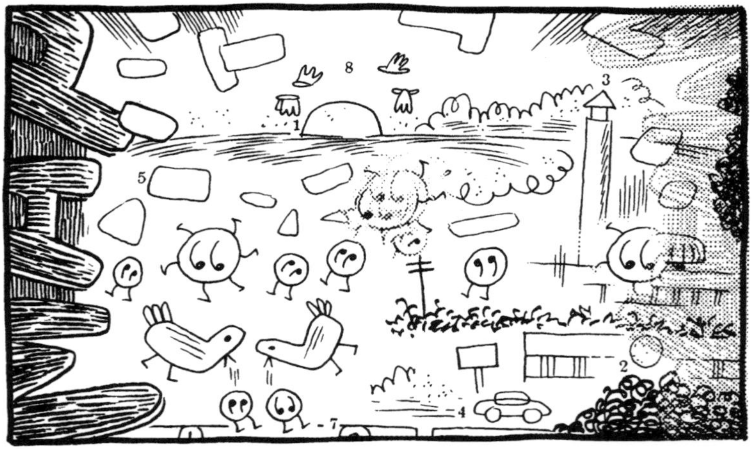
8
3
1
5
2
4
7

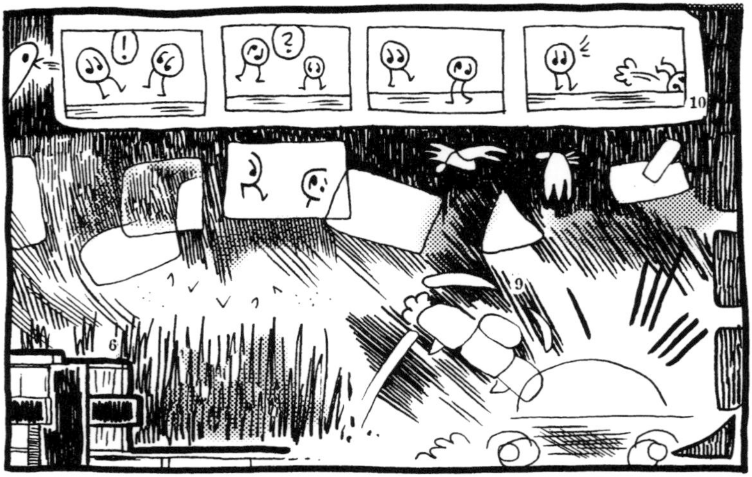
!
?
10
9
6

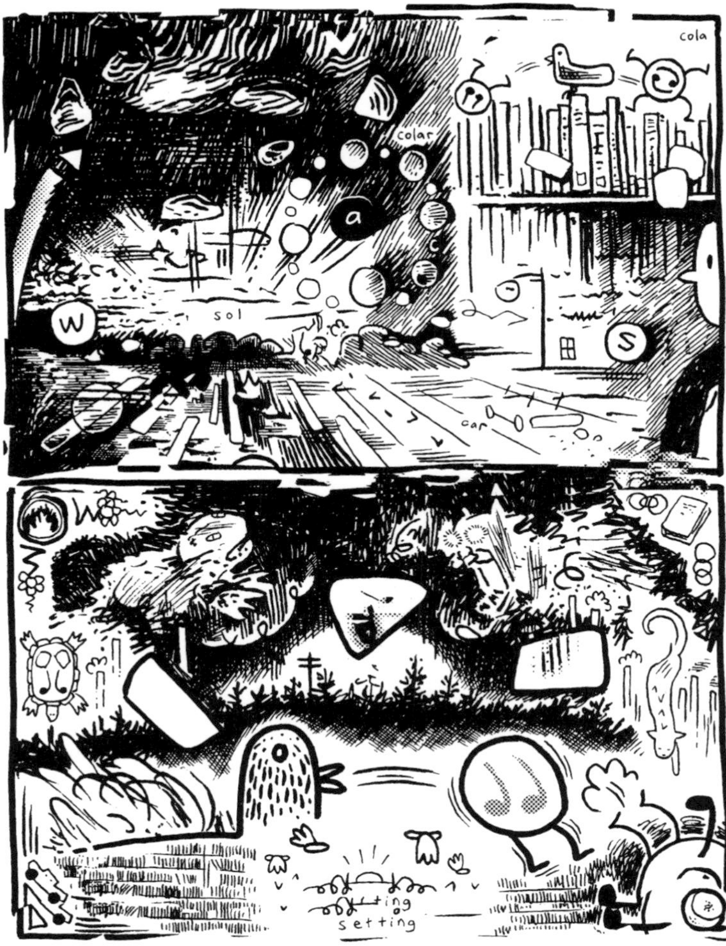

cola
colar
a
c
w
sol
s
car
setting

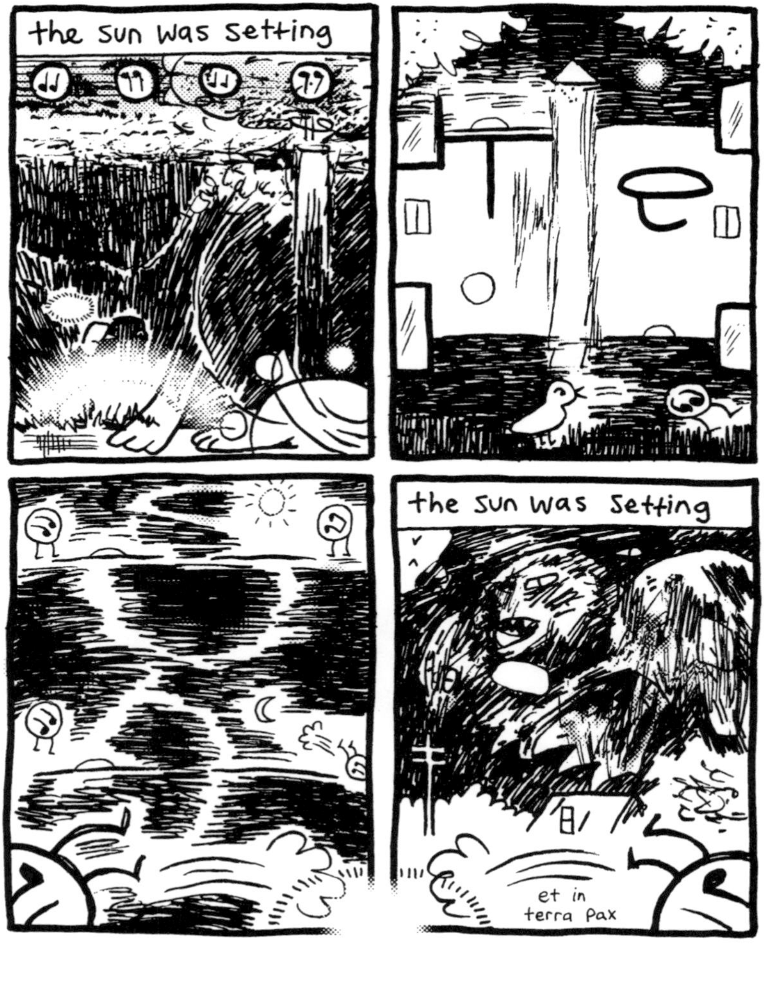
the sun was setting
the sun was setting
et in terra pax

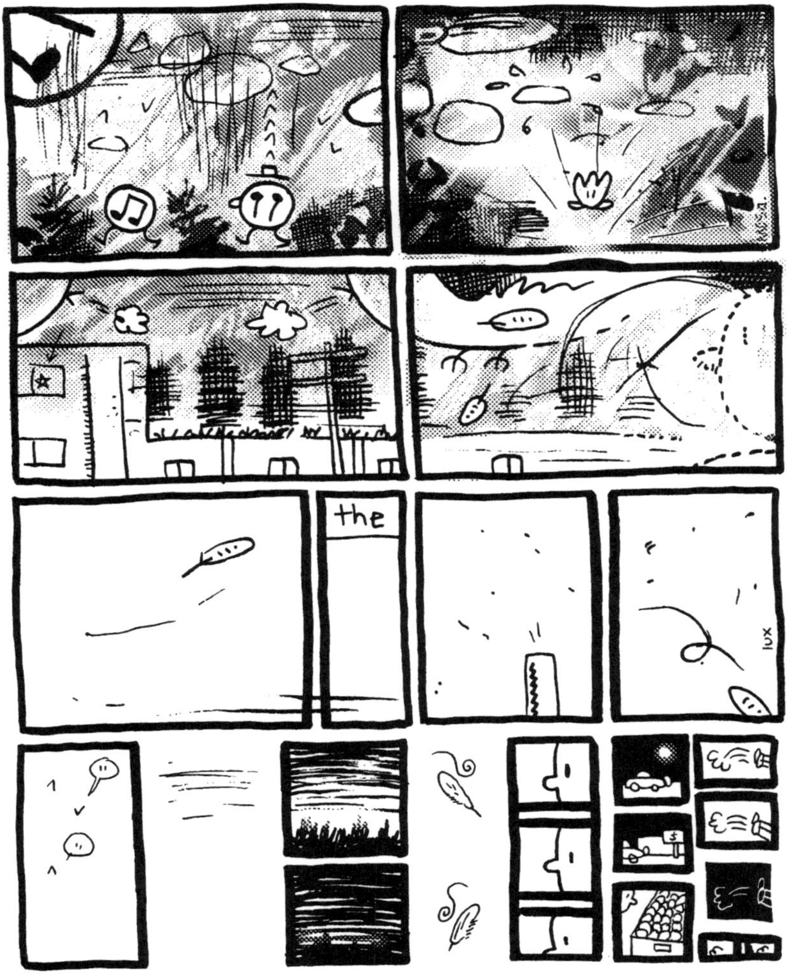
the
lux

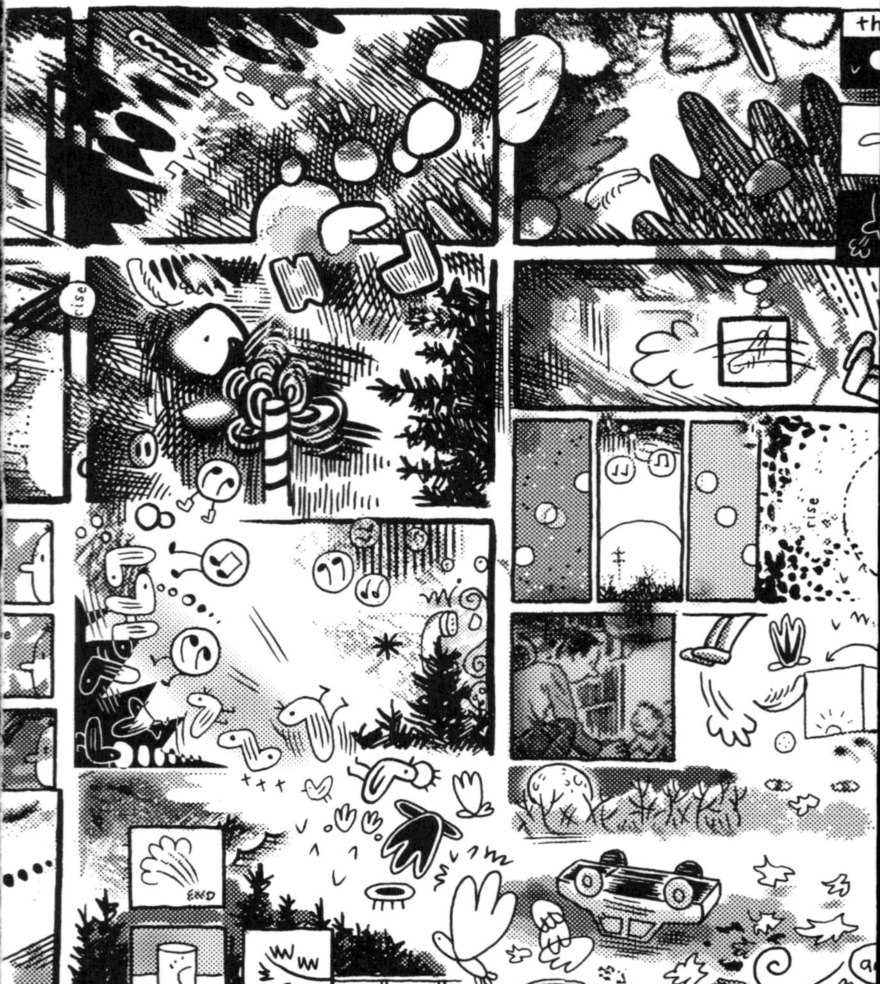
rise
rise

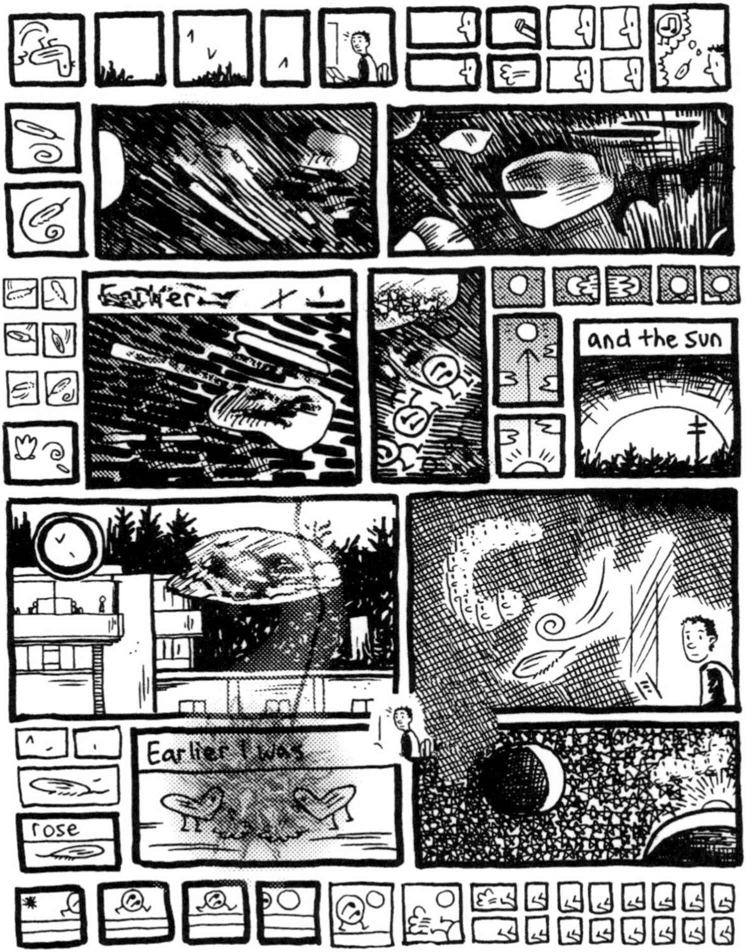
Earlier
and the sun
Earlier I was
rose

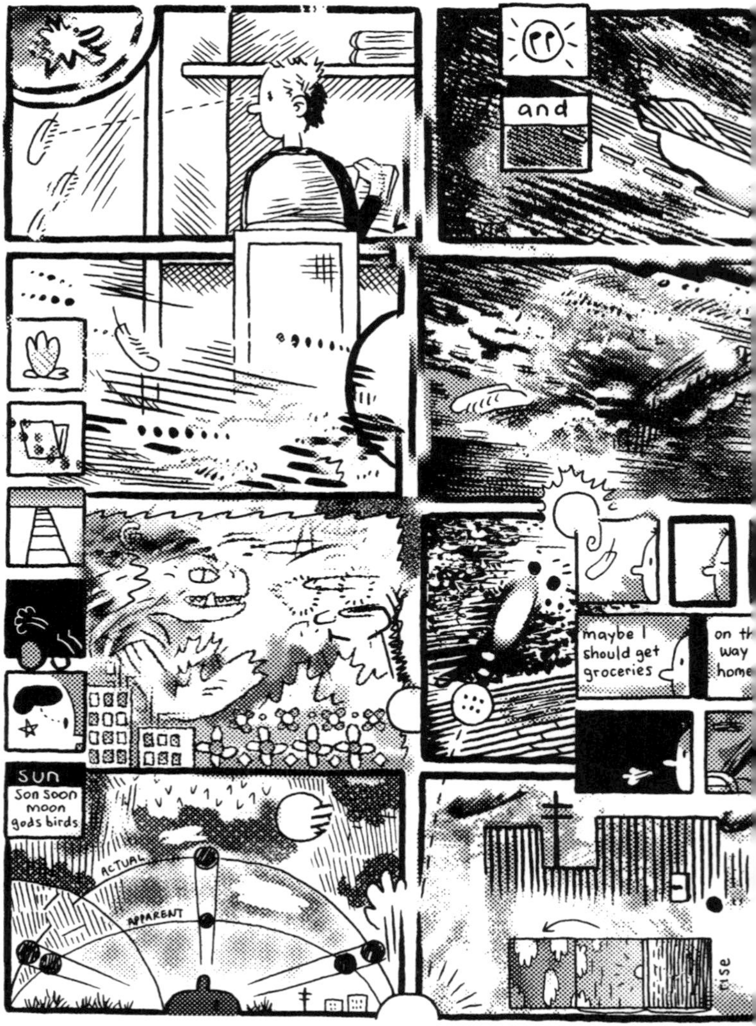
and
maybe I should get groceries
on th way home
sun
son soon moon gods birds
ACTUAL
APPARENT
rise

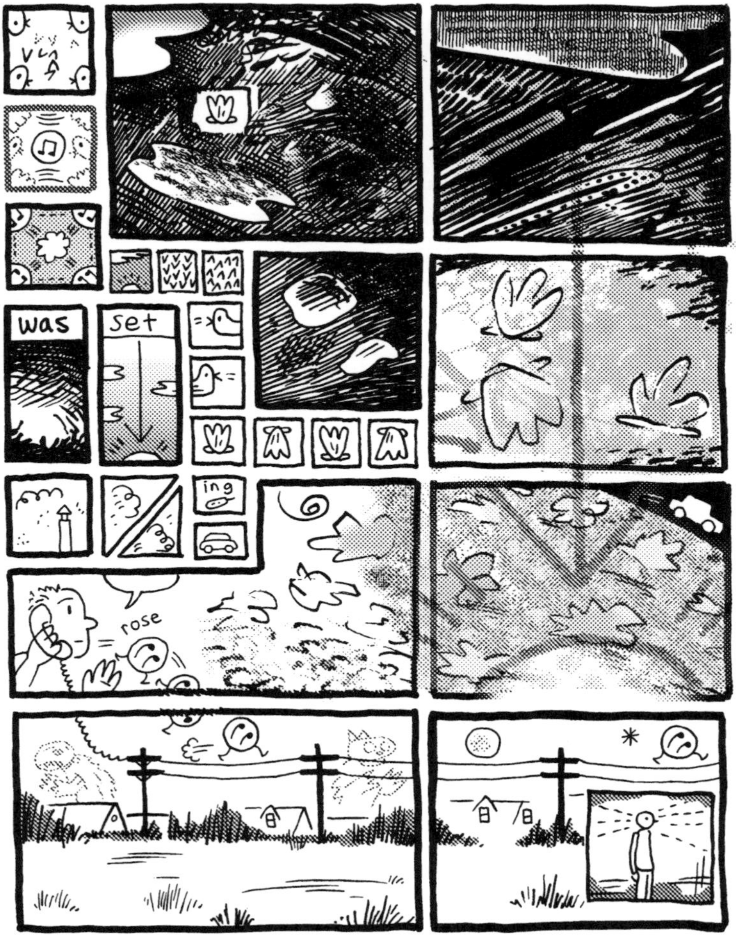
was
set
ing
rose

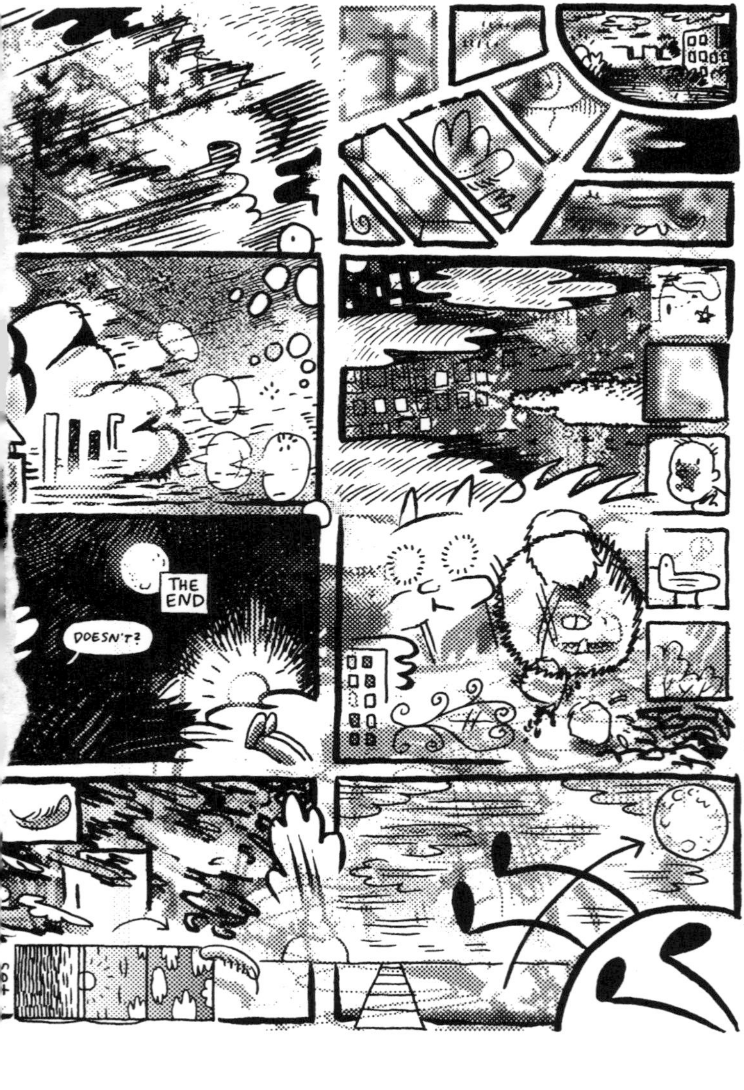
THE END
DOESN'T?

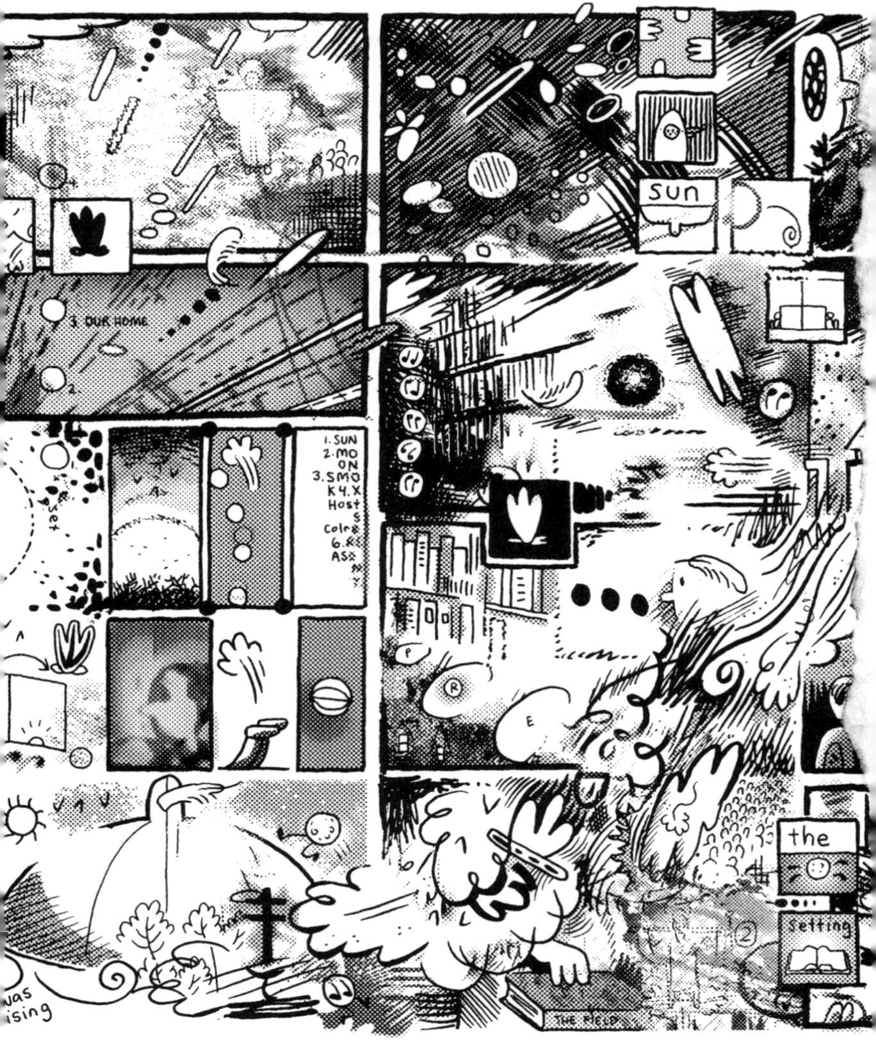
sun
3. OUR HOME
1. SUN
2. MO
ON
3. SMO
K 4. X
Host
s
Colr
set
P
R
E
V
the
setting
THE FIELD
was
ising

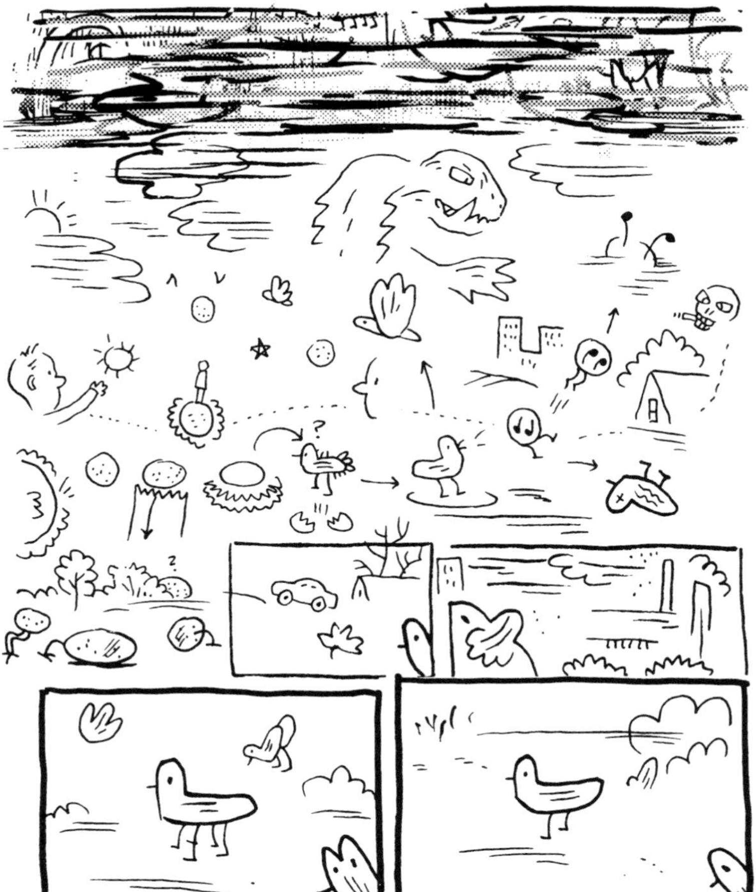

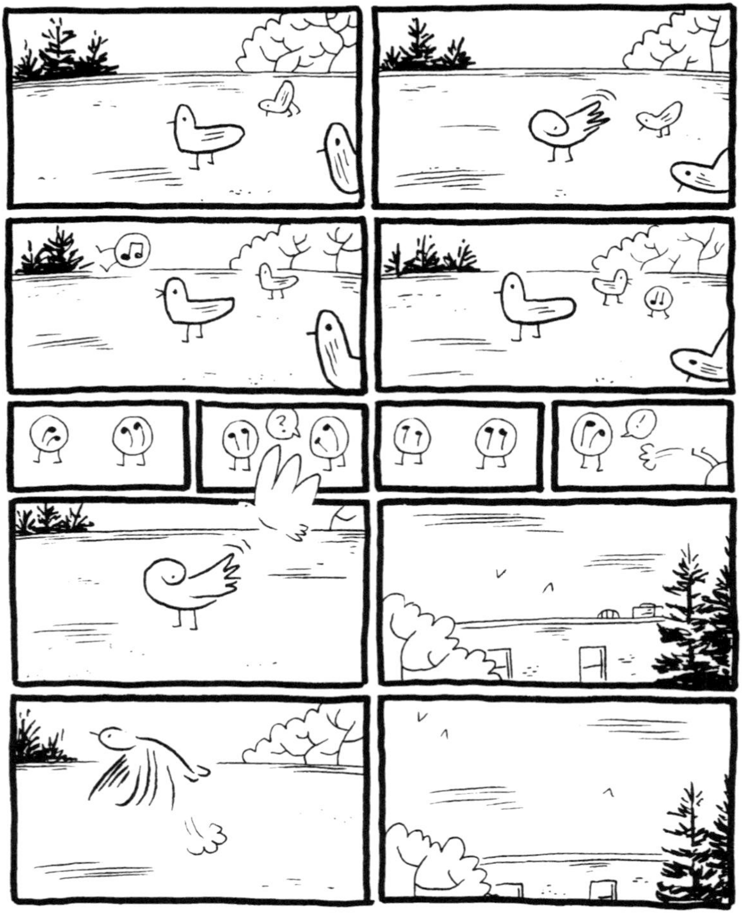
?
!

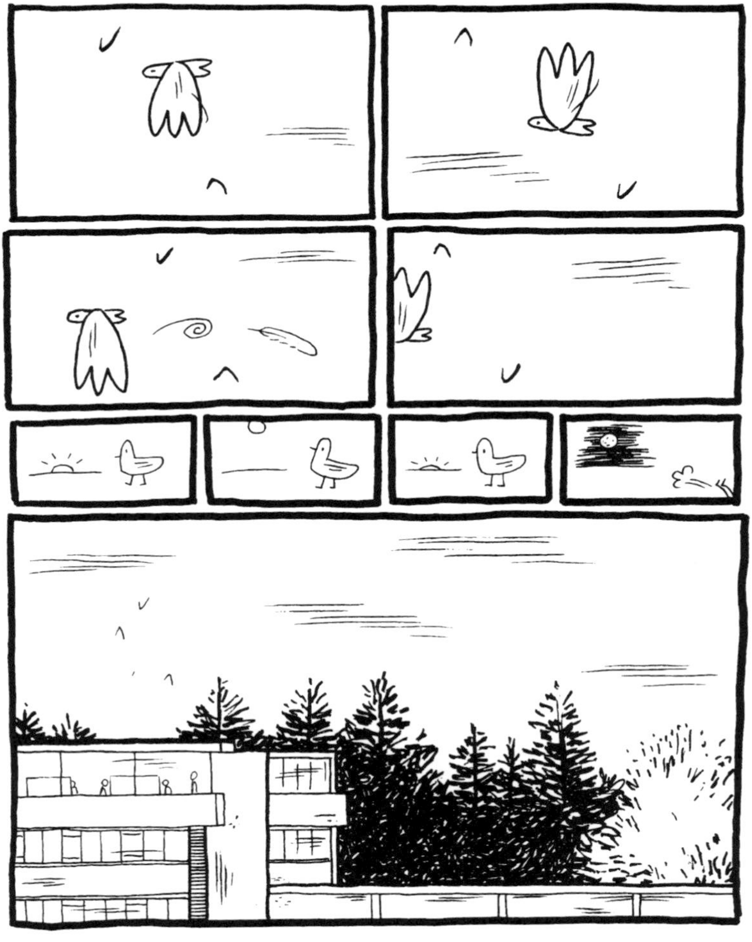

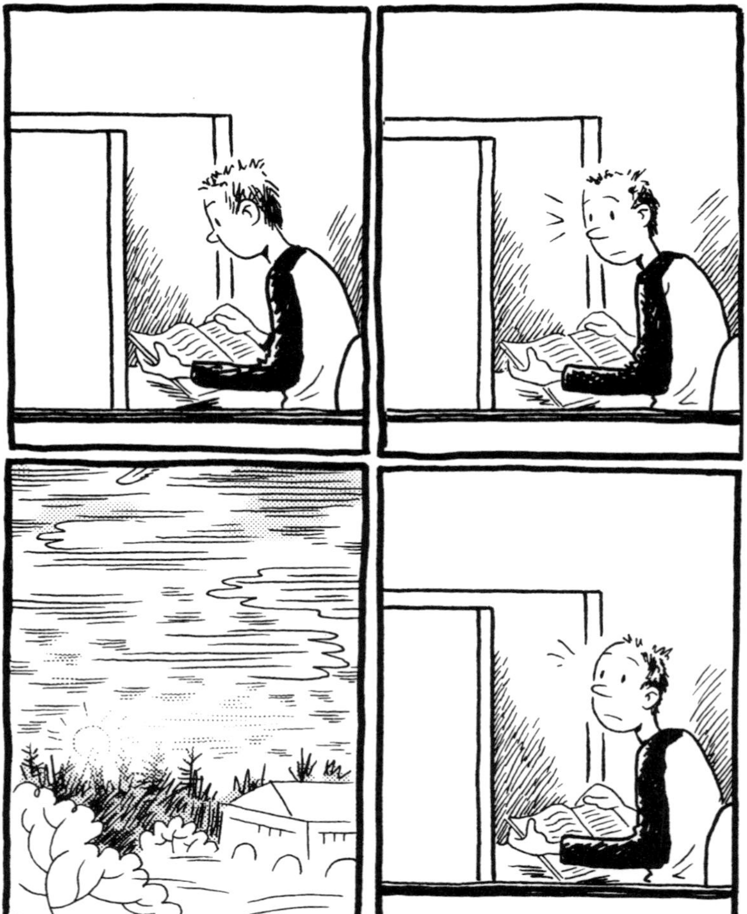

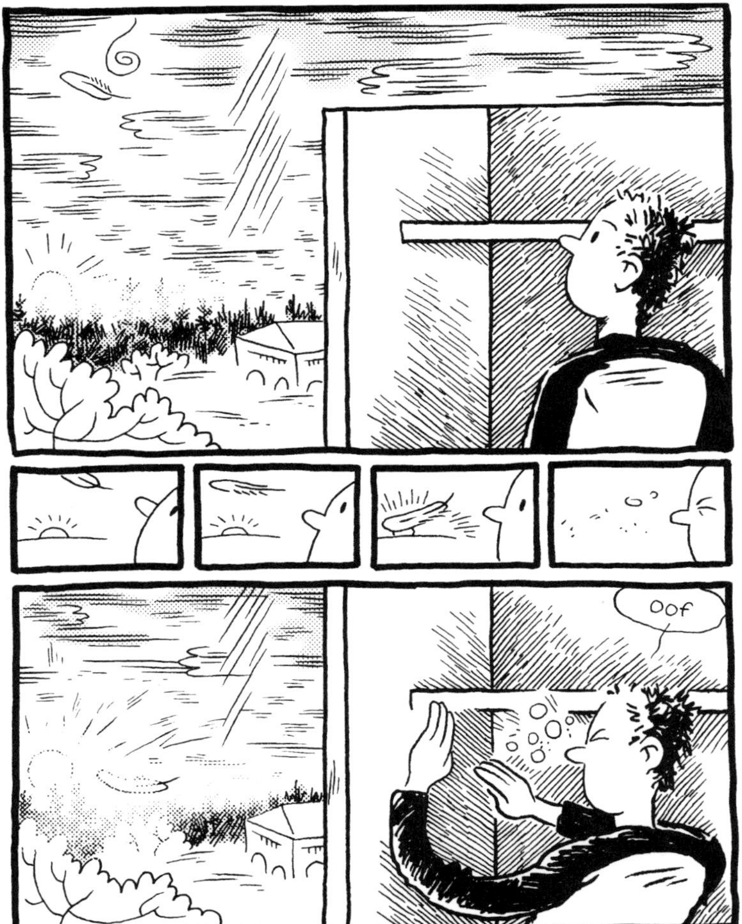
Oof

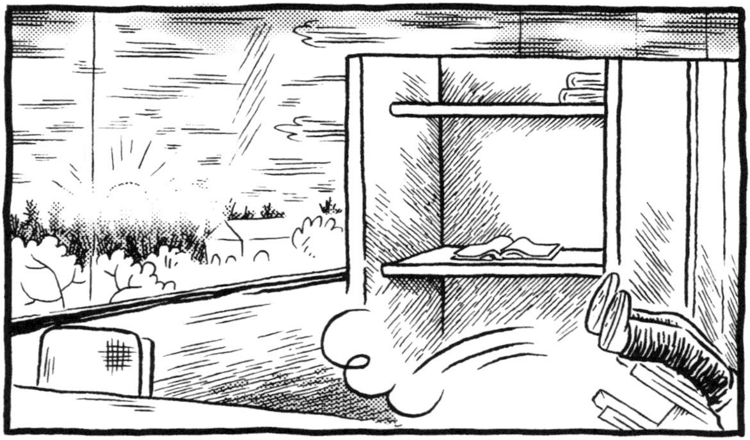

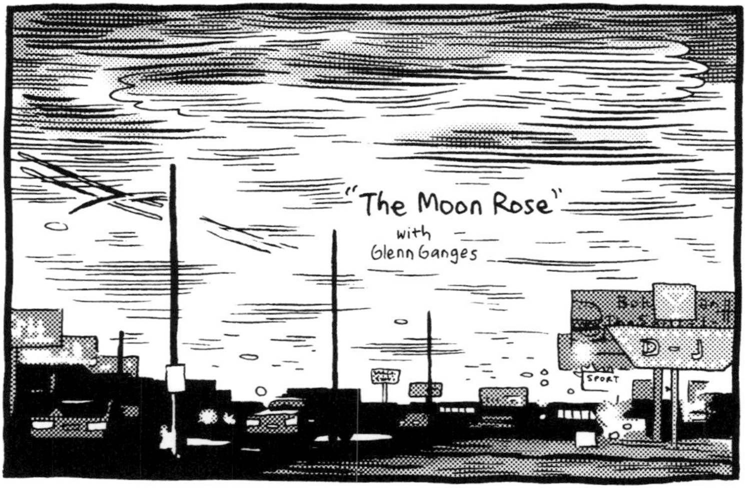
"The Moon Rose"
with
Glenn Ganges
D-J
SPORT

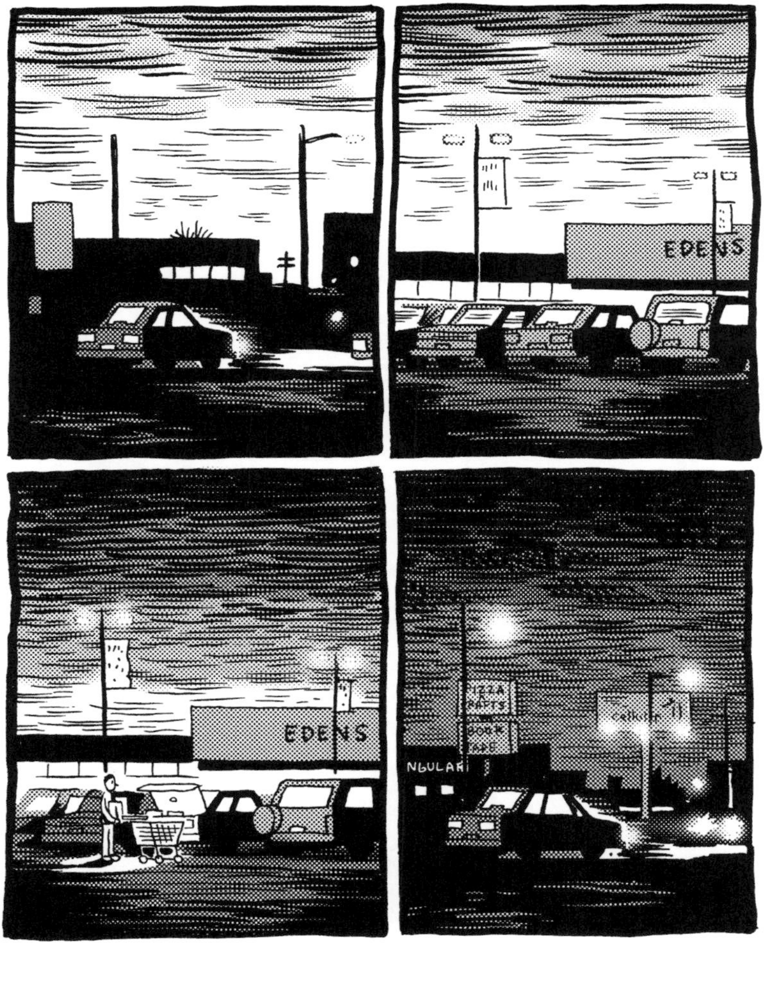
EDENS
EDENS
IZZA
BOOK
NGULAR

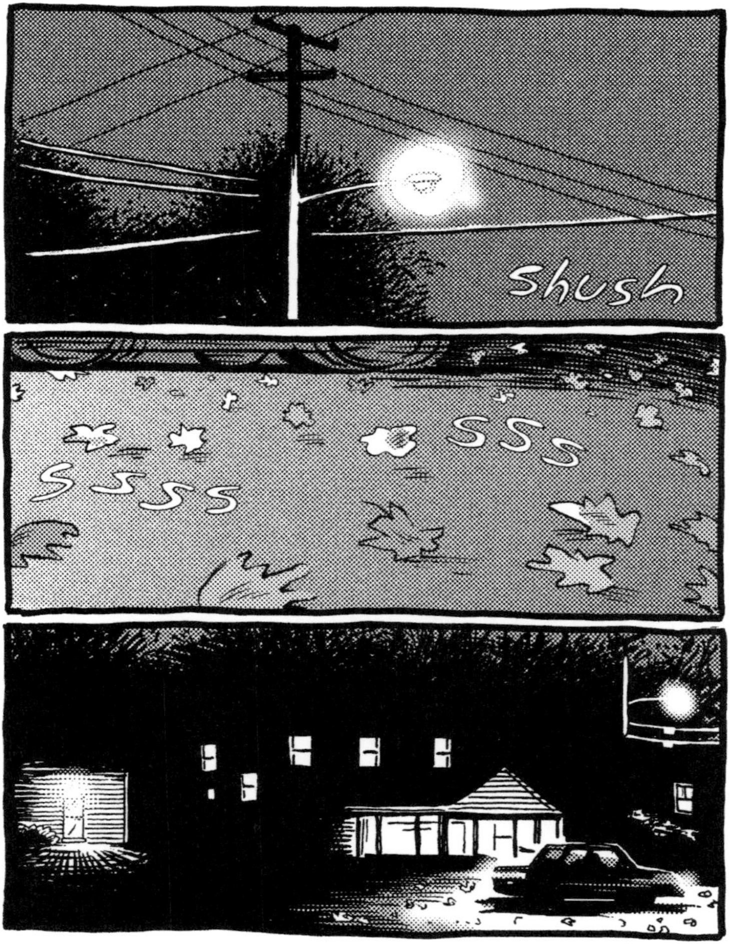
shush
SSS
SSSS

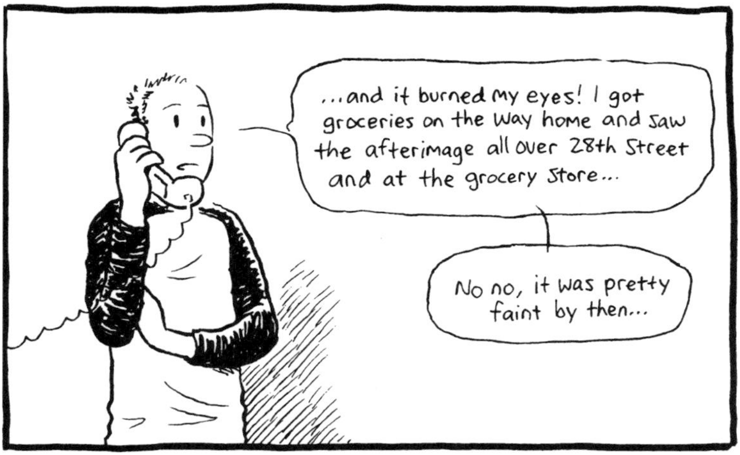
...and it burned my eyes! I got groceries on the way home and saw the afterimage all over 28th Street and at the grocery store...
No no, it was pretty faint by then...

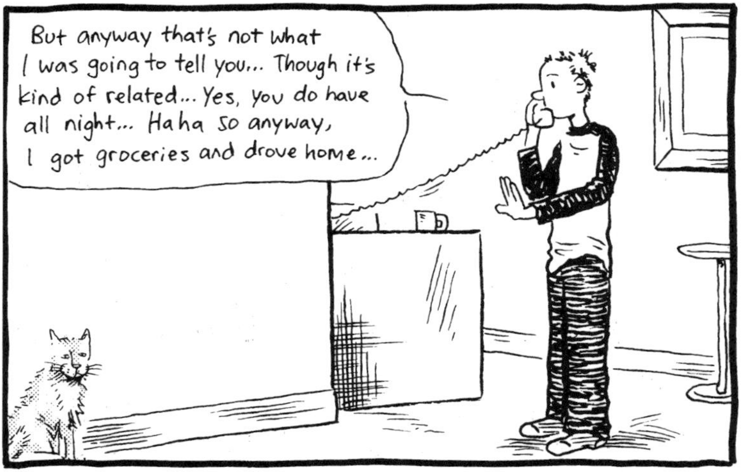
But anyway that's not what I was going to tell you... Though it's kind of related... Yes, you do have all night... Haha so anyway, I got groceries and drove home...

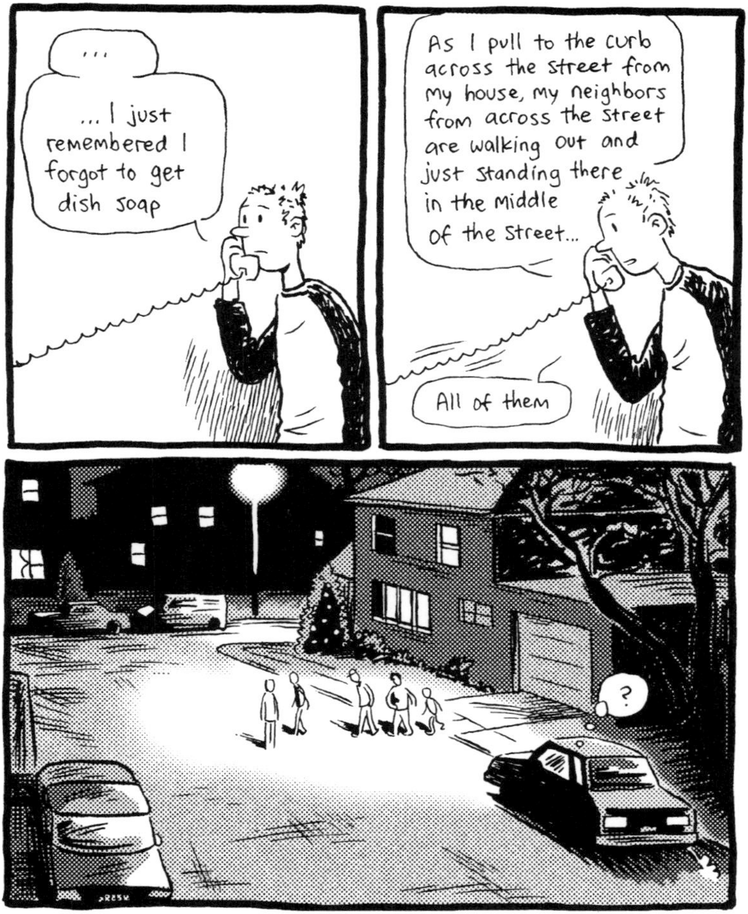
...
... I just remembered I forgot to get dish soap
As I pull to the curb across the street from my house, my neighbors from across the street are walking out and just standing there in the middle of the street...
All of them
?

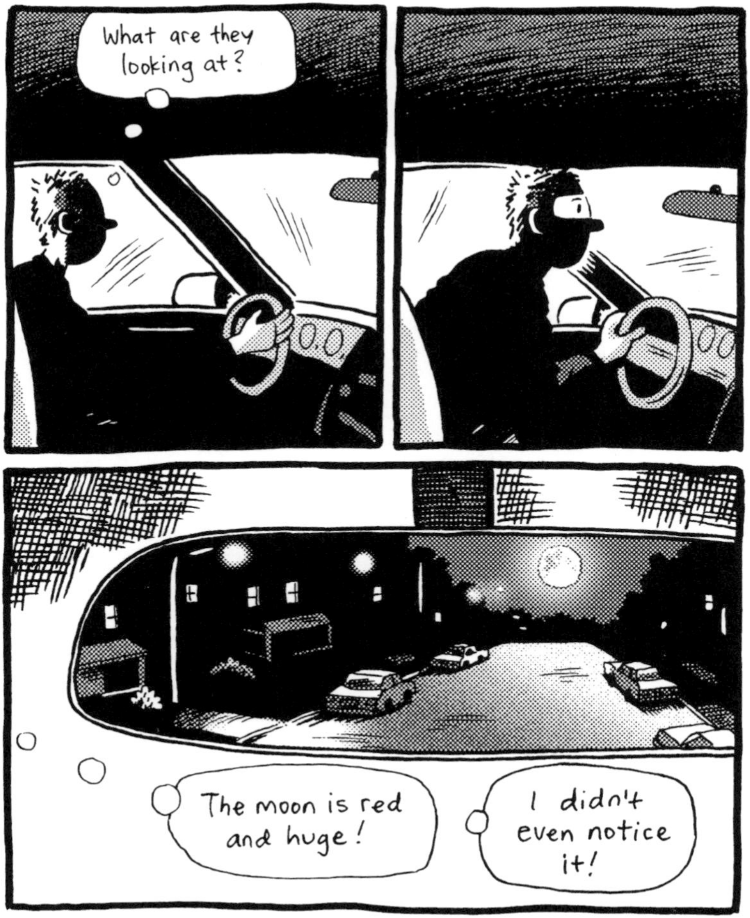
What are they looking at?
The moon is red and huge!
I didn't even notice it!

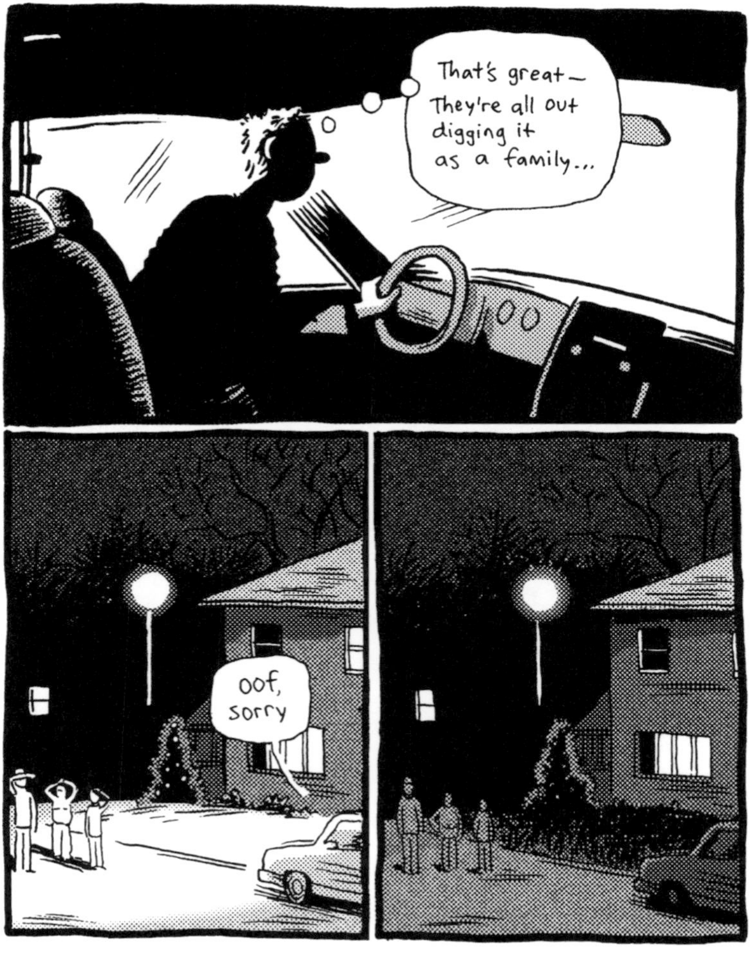
That's great—
They're all out
digging it
as a family...
oof,
sorry

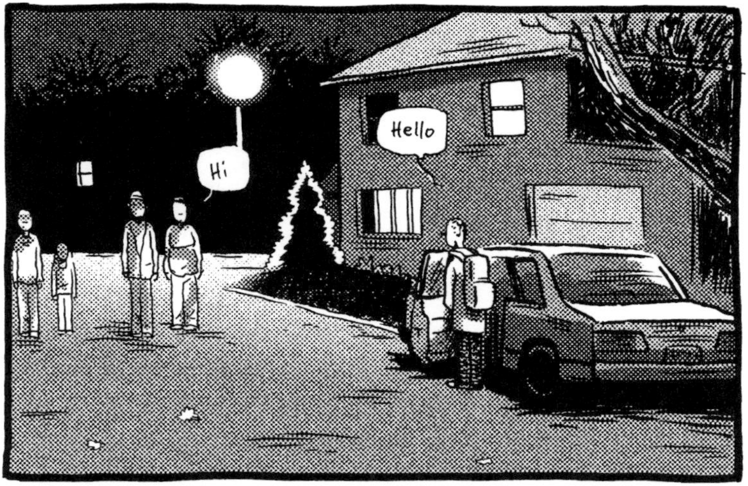
Hi
Hello

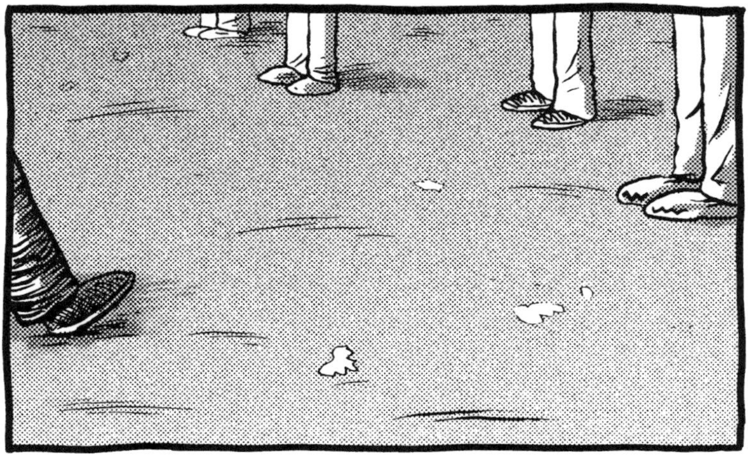

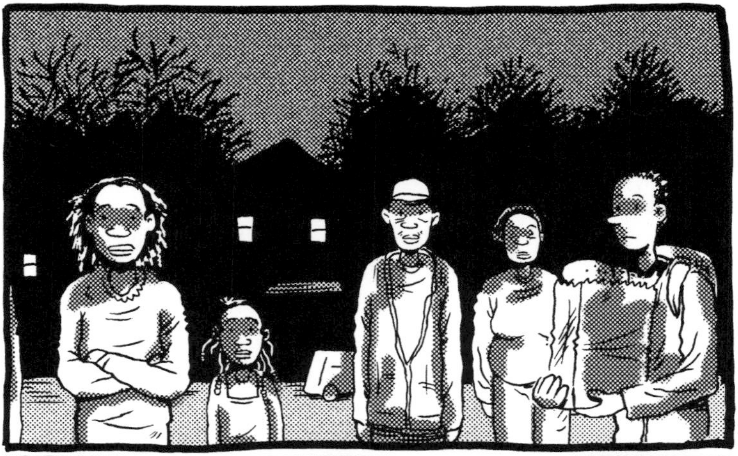

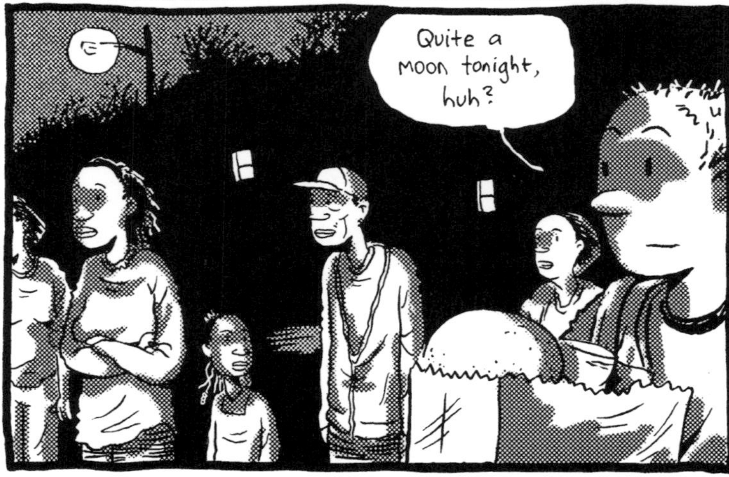
Quite a moon tonight, huh?

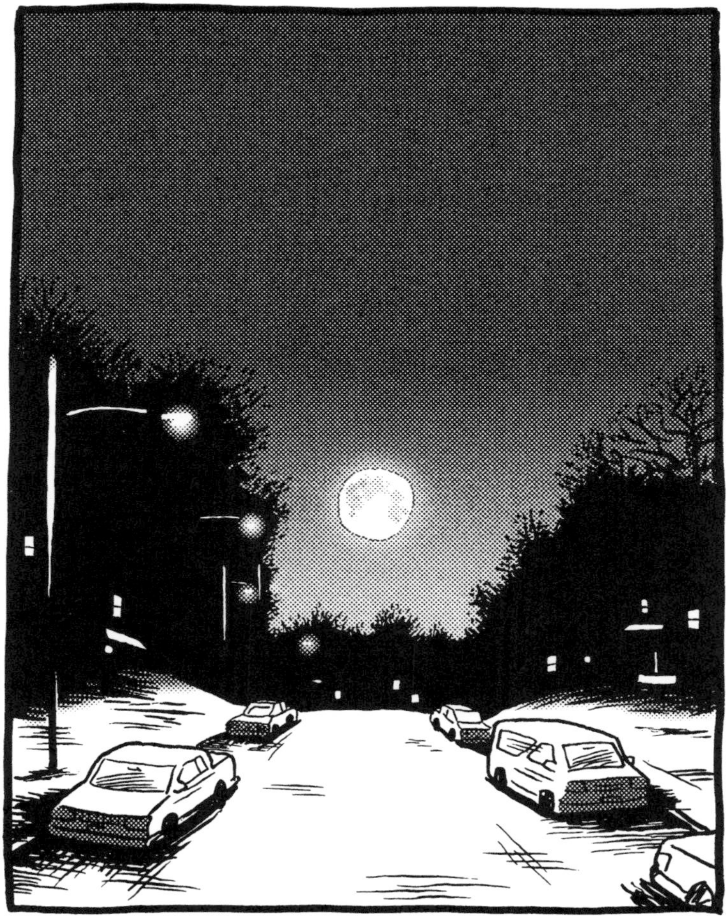

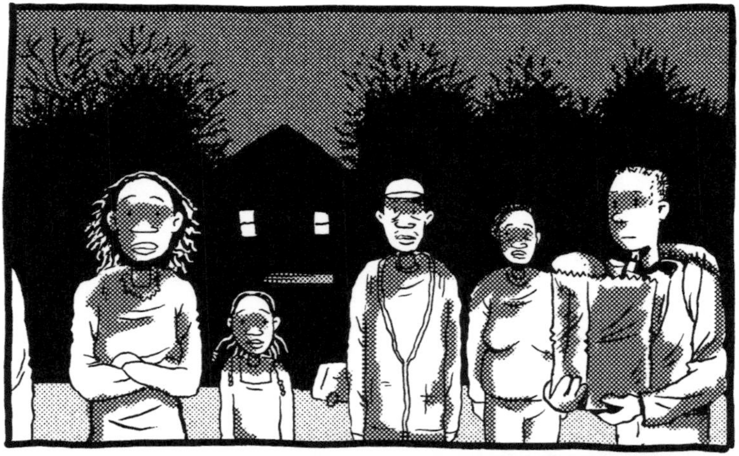

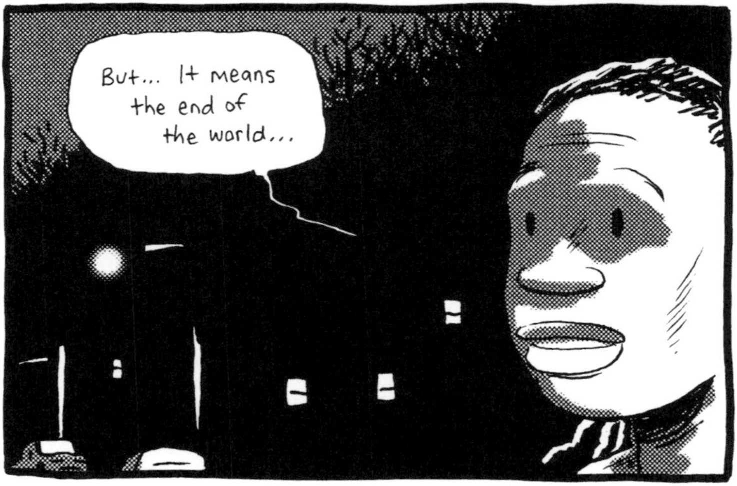
But... It means the end of the world...

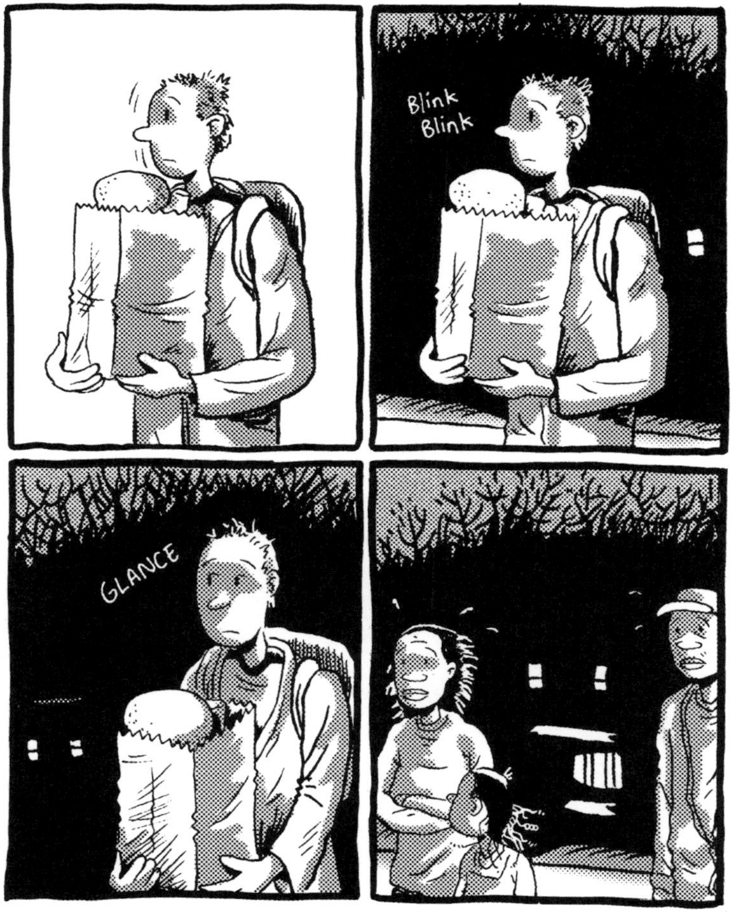
Blink
Blink
GLANCE

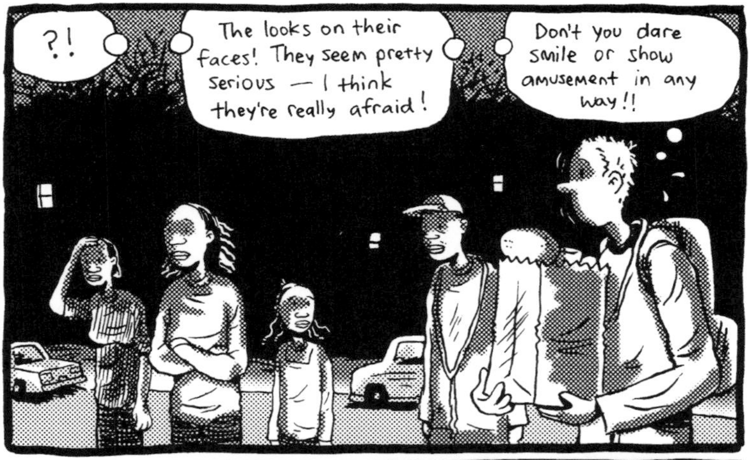
?!
The looks on their faces! They seem pretty serious — I think they're really afraid!
Don't you dare smile or show amusement in any way!!

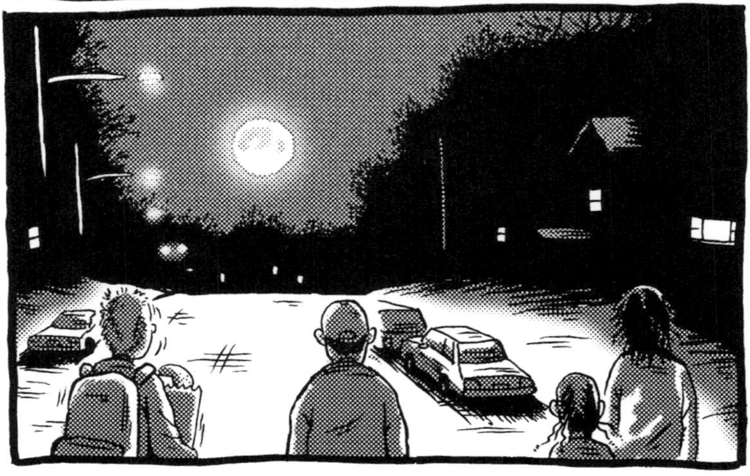

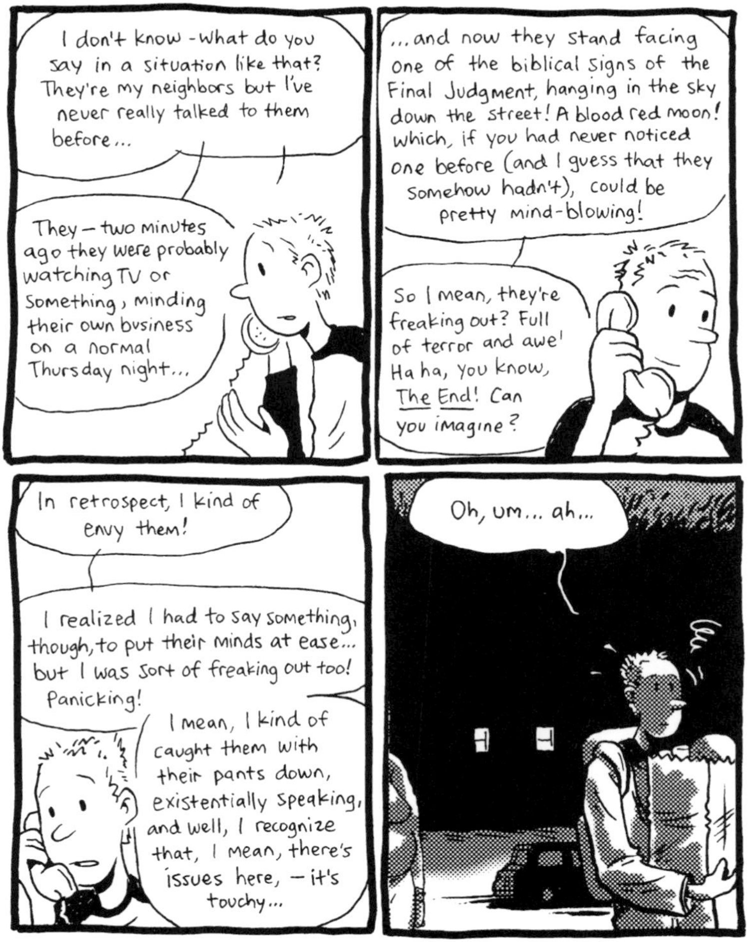
I don't know - what do you say in a situation like that? They're my neighbors but I've never really talked to them before...
They — two minutes ago they were probably watching TV or something, minding their own business on a normal Thursday night...
...and now they stand facing one of the biblical signs of the Final Judgment, hanging in the sky down the street! A blood red moon! which, if you had never noticed one before (and I guess that they somehow hadn't), could be pretty mind-blowing!
So I mean, they're freaking out? Full of terror and awe! Ha ha, you know, The End! Can you imagine?
In retrospect, I kind of envy them!
I realized I had to say something, though, to put their minds at ease... but I was sort of freaking out too! Panicking!
I mean, I kind of caught them with their pants down, existentially speaking, and well, I recognize that, I mean, there's issues here, — it's touchy...
Oh, um... ah...

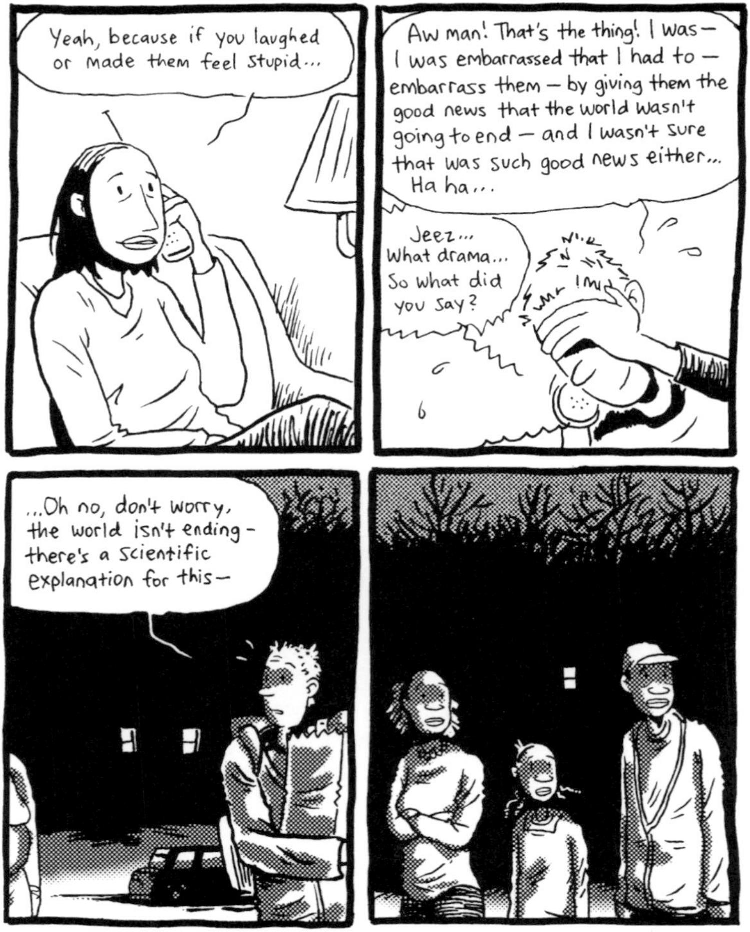
Yeah, because if you laughed or made them feel stupid...
Aw man! That's the thing! I was— I was embarrassed that I had to— embarrass them— by giving them the good news that the world wasn't going to end— and I wasn't sure that was such good news either... Ha ha...
Jeez... What drama... So what did you say?
...Oh no, don't worry, the world isn't ending— there's a scientific explanation for this—

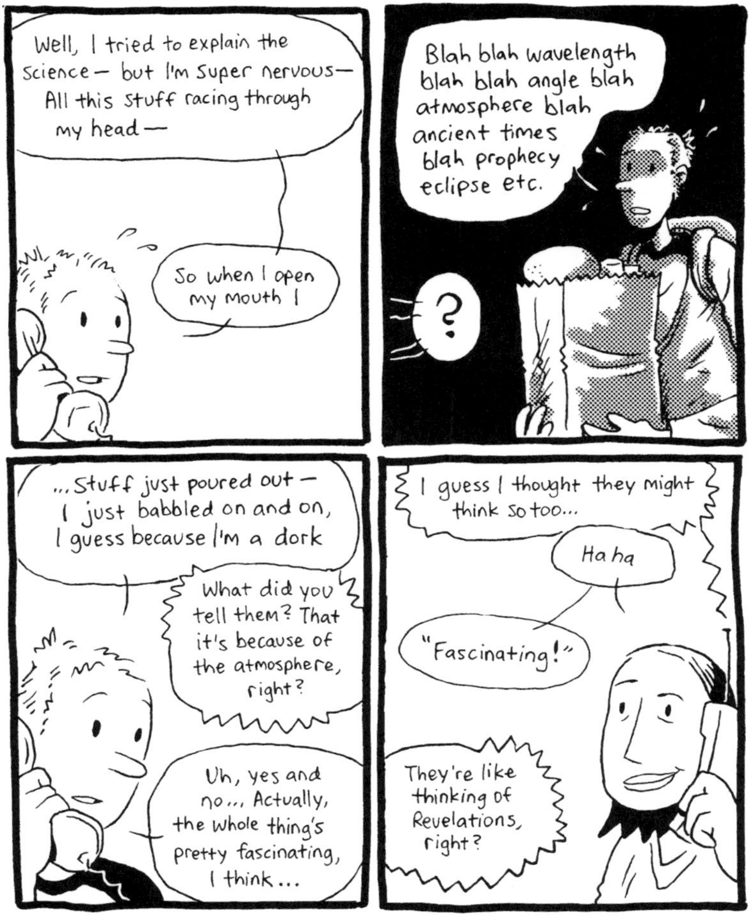
Well, I tried to explain the science— but I'm super nervous— All this stuff racing through my head—
So when I open my mouth I
Blah blah wavelength blah blah angle blah atmosphere blah ancient times blah prophecy eclipse etc.
?
...Stuff just poured out— I just babbled on and on, I guess because I'm a dork
What did you tell them? That it's because of the atmosphere, right?
Uh, yes and no... Actually, the whole thing's pretty fascinating, I think...
I guess I thought they might think so too...
Ha ha
"Fascinating!"
They're like thinking of Revelations, right?

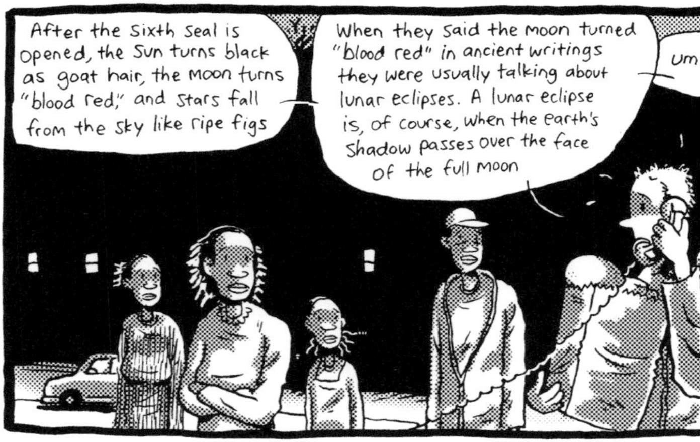
After the sixth seal is opened, the Sun turns black as goat hair, the moon turns "blood red," and stars fall from the sky like ripe figs
When they said the moon turned "blood red" in ancient writings they were usually talking about lunar eclipses. A lunar eclipse is, of course, when the earth's shadow passes over the face of the full moon
um...

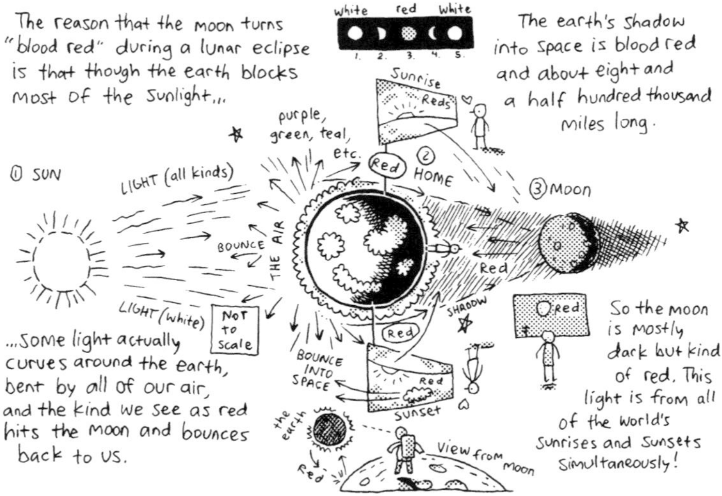
The reason that the moon turns "blood red" during a lunar eclipse is that though the earth blocks most of the sunlight...
white
red
white
1.
2.
3.
4.
5.
The earth's shadow into space is blood red and about eight and a half hundred thousand miles long.
Sunrise
Reds
purple, green, teal, etc.
Red
② HOME
③ Moon
① SUN
LIGHT (all kinds)
BOUNCE
THE AIR
Red
LIGHT (white)
Not to Scale
SHADOW
Red
...Some light actually curves around the earth, bent by all of our air, and the kind we see as red hits the moon and bounces back to us.
BOUNCE INTO SPACE
Red
Sunset
the earth
Red
View from moon
red
So the moon is mostly dark but kind of red. This light is from all of the world's sunrises and sunsets simultaneously!

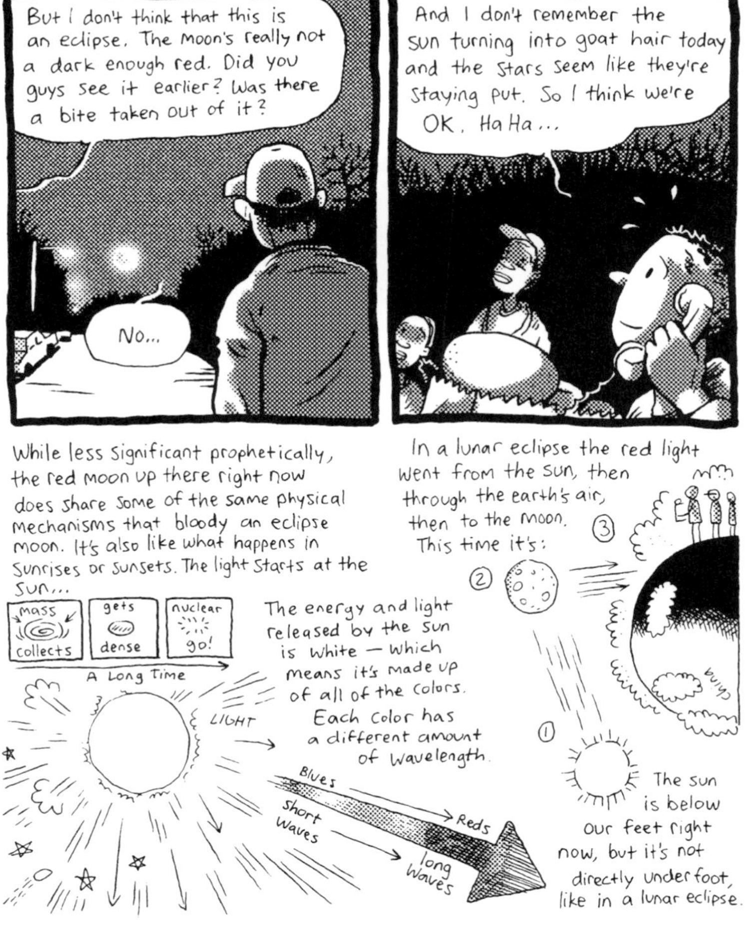

But I don't think that this is an eclipse. The moon's really not a dark enough red. Did you guys see it earlier? Was there a bite taken out of it?
No...
And I don't remember the sun turning into goat hair today and the stars seem like they're staying put. So I think we're OK. Ha Ha...
While less significant prophetically, the red moon up there right now does share some of the same physical mechanisms that bloody an eclipse moon. It's also like what happens in sunrises or sunsets. The light starts at the sun...
mass collects
gets dense
nuclear go!
A Long Time
LIGHT
The energy and light released by the sun is white — which means it's made up of all of the colors.
Each color has a different amount of wavelength.
Blues
Short Waves
Reds
long Waves
In a lunar eclipse the red light went from the sun, then through the earth's air, then to the moon.
This time it's:
①
②
③
China
The sun is below our feet right now, but it's not directly underfoot, like in a lunar eclipse.

So the sunlight, still white, hits the moon and reflects off it towards us. What happens next depends on you and the moon's relation.

At its zenith, the moon's light passes through less air than when it's on the horizon, so the moon looks white. When the moonlight passes through more air, colors with little wavelengths get bounced but reds get through.

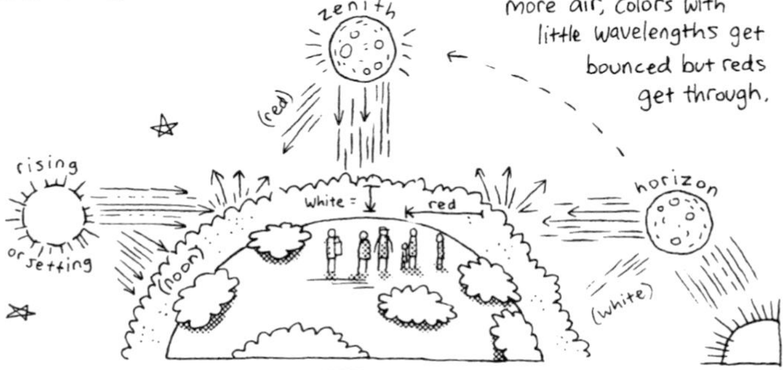

zenith
(red)
rising
or setting
(noon)
white =
red
horizon
(white)

In the spring, plants about to reproduce shoot loads of pollen into the atmosphere. In the fall, farmers kick up dust and old pollen during harvest.

Cars, smoke stacks and volcanoes add tons of dust and soot to the air. These particles are behind the scattering of light from space.

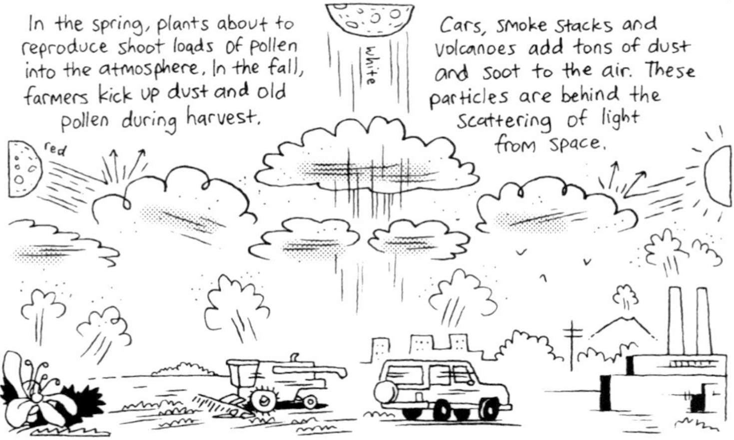

white
red

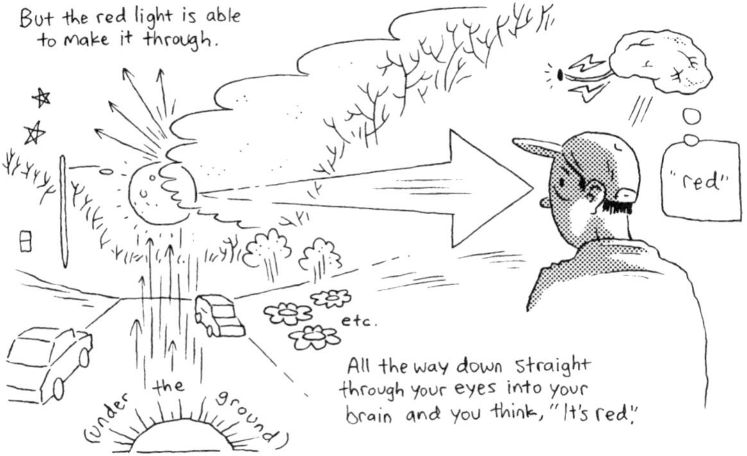

But the red light is able to make it through.
"red"
etc.
(under the ground)
All the way down straight through your eyes into your brain and you think, "It's red."

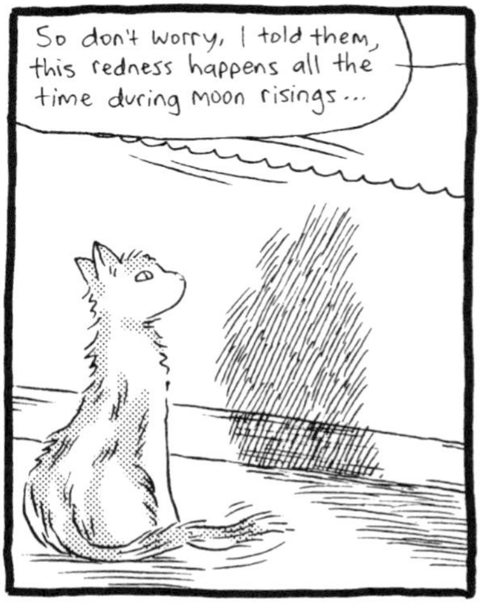

So don't worry, I told them, this redness happens all the time during moon risings...

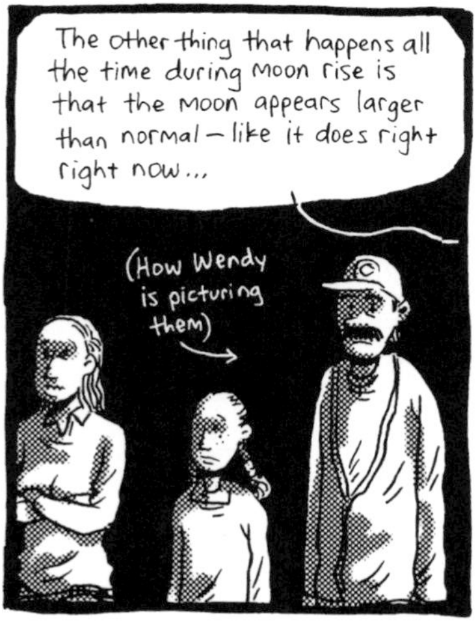

The other thing that happens all the time during moon rise is that the moon appears larger than normal—like it does right right now...
(How Wendy is picturing them)

Some people think the moon looks bigger because it somehow comes closer when it's on the horizon. But this is wrong. The moon is always about a quarter million miles away. Its orbit is circular.

A lot of people, Ptolemy included, think it's the atmosphere. Moon light at the horizon angle of passing through so much air makes the moon red, so people think it magnifies it too. But if you study the angles it's actually the opposite.

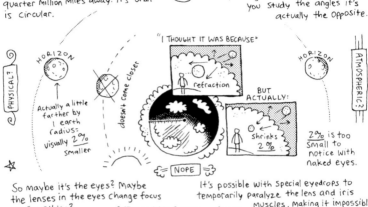

"I THOUGHT IT WAS BECAUSE"

PHYSICAL?

HORIZON

Actually a little farther by 1 earth radius= visually 2% smaller

doesn't come closer

refraction

BUT ACTUALLY:

shrinks 2%

2% is too small to notice with naked eyes.

HORIZON

ATMOSPHERIC?

NOPE

So maybe it's the eyes? Maybe the lenses in the eyes change focus or something?

RETINAL IMAGE

(UPSIDE DOWN

BUT BRAIN FIXES)

It's not this either.

It's possible with special eyedrops to temporarily paralyze the lens and iris muscles, making it impossible for the retinal image to change size. Also a condition named presbyopia sometimes afflicts older adults and has the same effect. In both cases, the moon size change is still seen.

Scientists have measured the little circle of light on the back of people's eyeballs for both moons and they're the same size.

EYES?

HORIZON

ZENITH

0.15mm

PARALYZED EYES

PRESBYOPIA

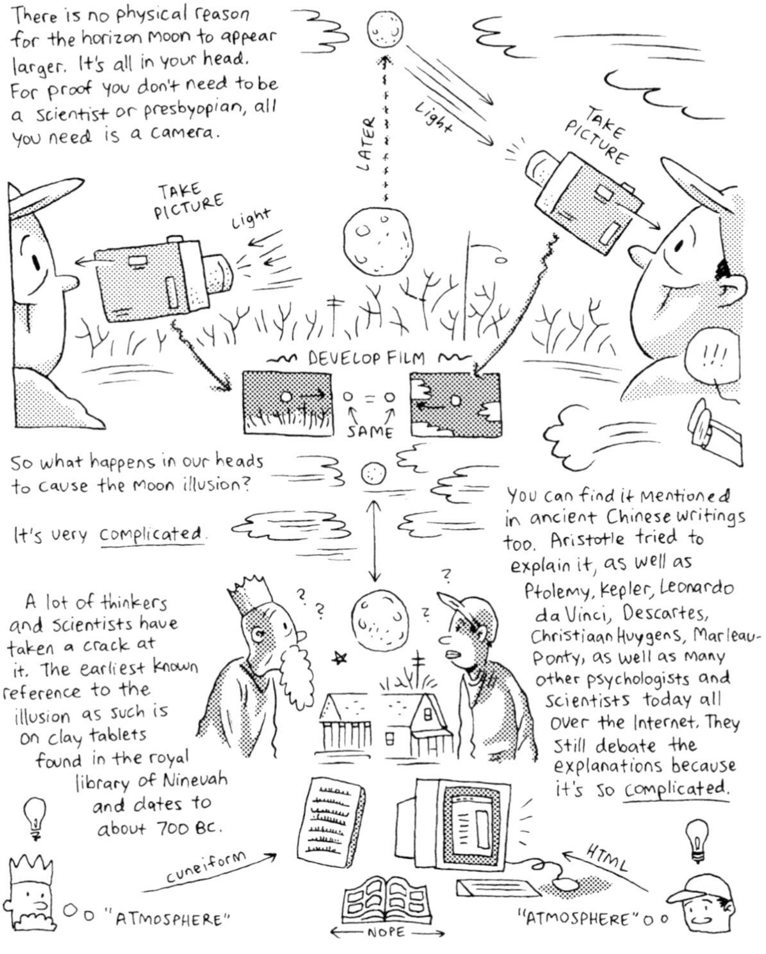
There is no physical reason for the horizon Moon to appear larger. It's all in your head. For proof you don't need to be a scientist or presbyopian, all you need is a camera.
Light
LATER
TAKE PICTURE
TAKE PICTURE
Light
!!!
DEVELOP FILM
SAME
So what happens in our heads to cause the Moon illusion?
It's very complicated.
You can find it mentioned in ancient Chinese writings too. Aristotle tried to explain it, as well as Ptolemy, Kepler, Leonardo da Vinci, Descartes, Christiaan Huygens, Marleau-Ponty, as well as many other psychologists and scientists today all over the Internet. They still debate the explanations because it's so complicated.
A lot of thinkers and scientists have taken a crack at it. The earliest known reference to the illusion as such is on clay tablets found in the royal library of Ninevah and dates to about 700 BC.
cuneiform
HTML
"ATMOSPHERE"
"ATMOSPHERE"
NOPE

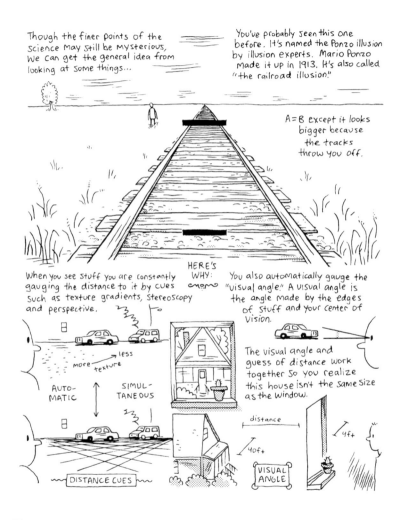

Though the finer points of the science may still be mysterious, we can get the general idea from looking at some things...

You've probably seen this one before. It's named the Ponzo illusion by illusion experts. Mario Ponzo made it up in 1913. It's also called "the railroad illusion."

A=B except it looks bigger because the tracks throw you off.

HERE'S WHY:

When you see stuff you are constantly gauging the distance to it by cues such as texture gradients, stereoscopy and perspective.

You also automatically gauge the "visual angle." A visual angle is the angle made by the edges of stuff and your center of vision.

The visual angle and guess of distance work together so you realize this house isn't the same size as the window.

more texture → less

AUTO-MATIC

SIMUL-TANEOUS

DISTANCE CUES

distance

40ft

VISUAL ANGLE

4ft

Without your noticing it, the world makes sense as far as this: the visual angle etc. of an object is determined by its context and vice versa, so as to orient one's self in the theater of objects.

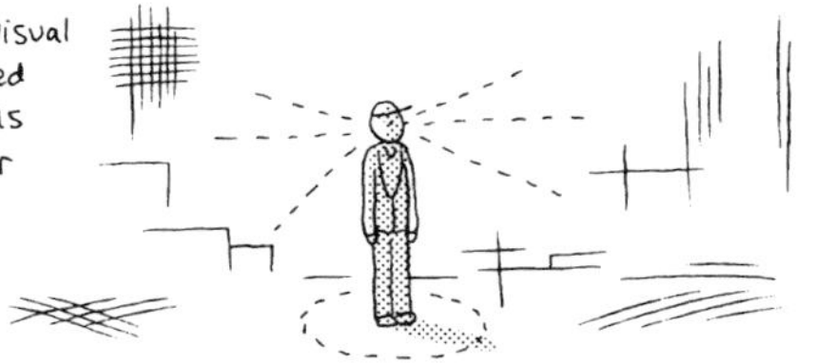

You can pretty much count on this stuff. If two objects have the same visual angle (visual size), but different distances, your brain knows they are different sizes even without thinking about it.

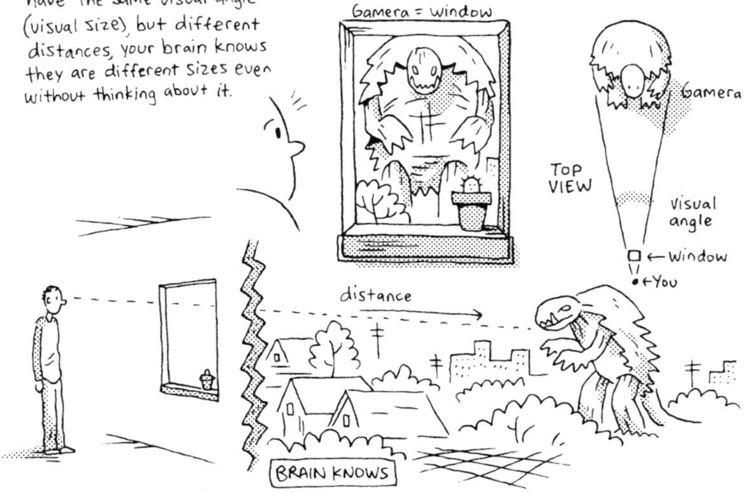

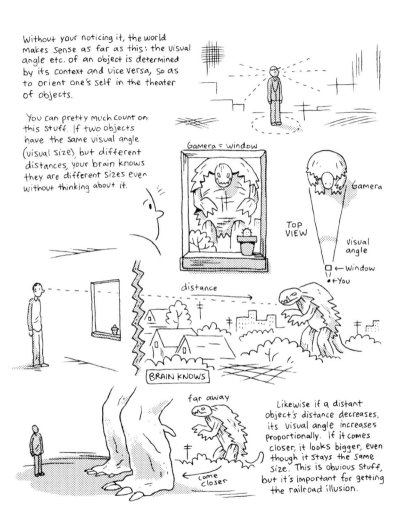

Gamera = window
Gamera
TOP VIEW
visual angle
← window
← You
distance
BRAIN KNOWS

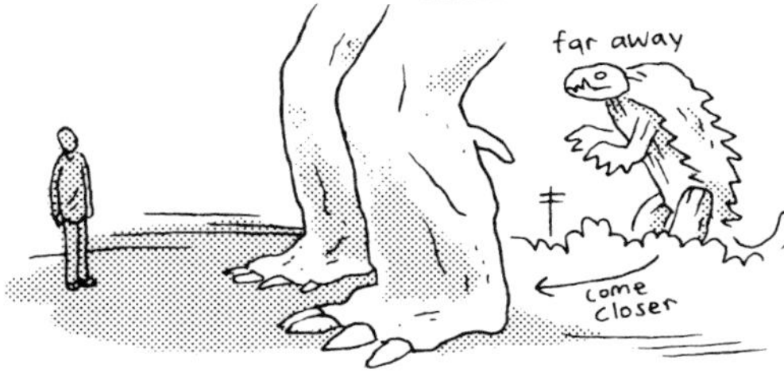

far away
come closer

Likewise if a distant object's distance decreases, its visual angle increases proportionally. If it comes closer, it looks bigger, even though it stays the same size. This is obvious stuff, but it's important for getting the railroad illusion.

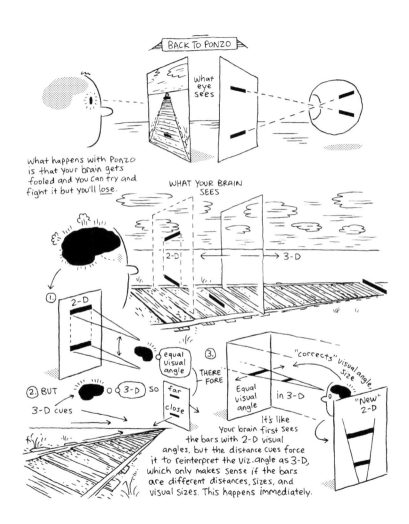

What eye sees

what happens with Ponzo is that your brain gets fooled and you can try and fight it but you'll <u>lose</u>.

WHAT YOUR BRAIN SEES

2-D ← → 3-D

(1.)

2-D

equal visual angle

(2.) BUT

3-D cues

THERE FORE

far
close

(3.)

"corrects" visual angle size

Equal visual angle in 3-D

"New" 2-D

It's like your brain first sees the bars with 2-D visual angles, but the distance cues force it to reinterpret the viz. angle as 3-D, which only makes sense if the bars are different distances, sizes, and visual sizes. This happens immediately.

Something like this happens in many optical illusions.

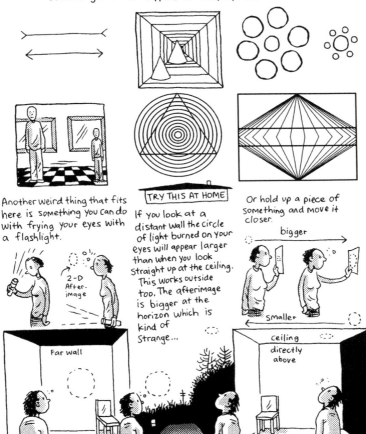

Another weird thing that fits here is something you can do with frying your eyes with a flashlight.

2-D After-image

Far wall

TRY THIS AT HOME

If you look at a distant wall the circle of light burned on your eyes will appear larger than when you look straight up at the ceiling. This works outside too. The afterimage is bigger at the horizon which is kind of strange...

Or hold up a piece of something and move it closer.

bigger

smaller

ceiling directly above

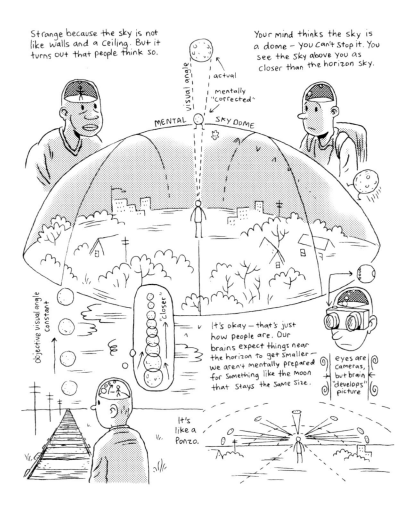

Strange because the sky is not like walls and a ceiling. But it turns out that people think so.

Your mind thinks the sky is a dome — you can't stop it. You see the sky above you as closer than the horizon sky.

actual

mentally "corrected"

visual angle

MENTAL SKY DOME

objective visual angle constant

"closer"

It's okay — that's just how people are. Our brains expect things near the horizon to get smaller — we aren't mentally prepared for something like the moon that stays the same size.

eyes are cameras, but brain "develops" picture

It's like a Ponzo.

94

You might see two objections:

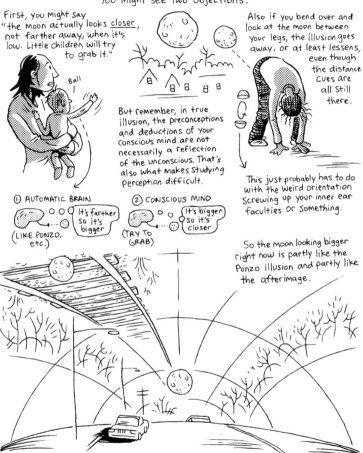

First, you might say "the moon actually looks <u>closer</u>, not farther away, when it's low. Little children will try to grab it."

Ball

Also if you bend over and look at the moon between your legs, the illusion goes away, or at least lessens, even though the distance cues are all still there.

But remember, in true illusion, the preconceptions and deductions of your conscious mind are not necessarily a reflection of the unconscious. That's also what makes studying perception difficult.

This just probably has to do with the weird orientation screwing up your inner ear faculties or something.

① AUTOMATIC BRAIN
It's farther so it's bigger
(LIKE PONZO, etc.)

② CONSCIOUS MIND
It's bigger so it's closer
(TRY TO GRAB)

So the moon looking bigger right now is partly like the Ponzo illusion and partly like the afterimage.

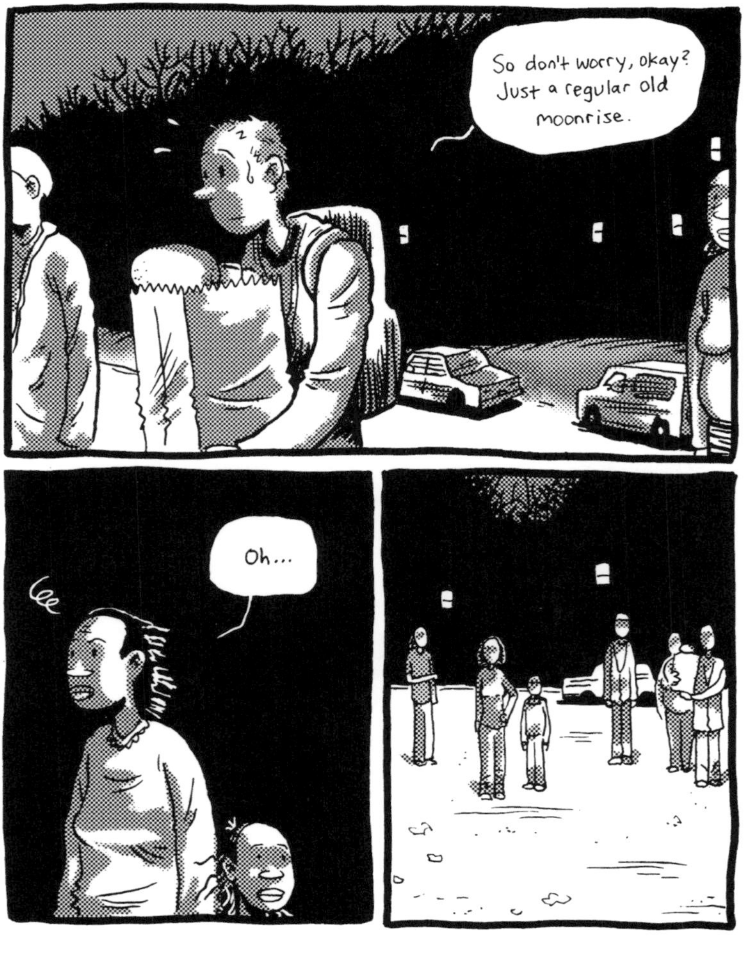
So don't worry, okay? Just a regular old moonrise.
Oh...

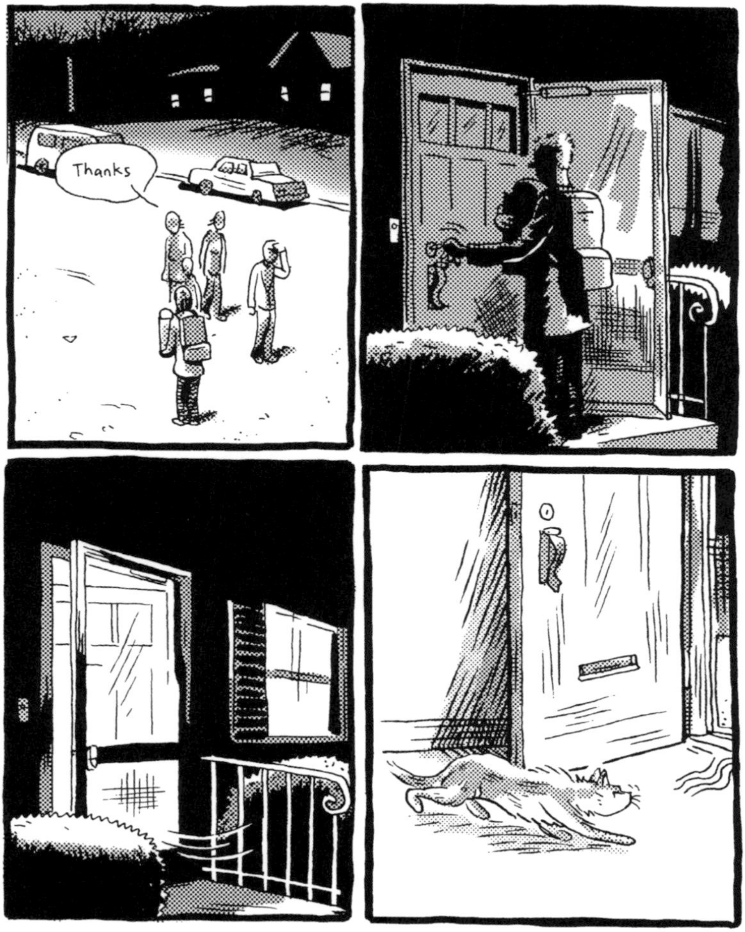
Thanks

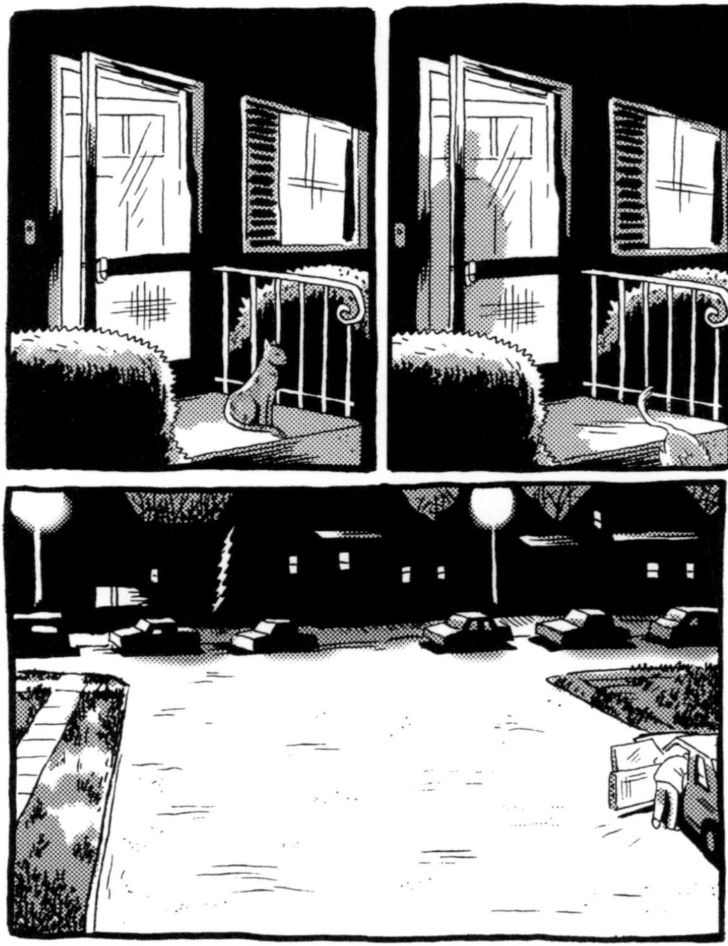

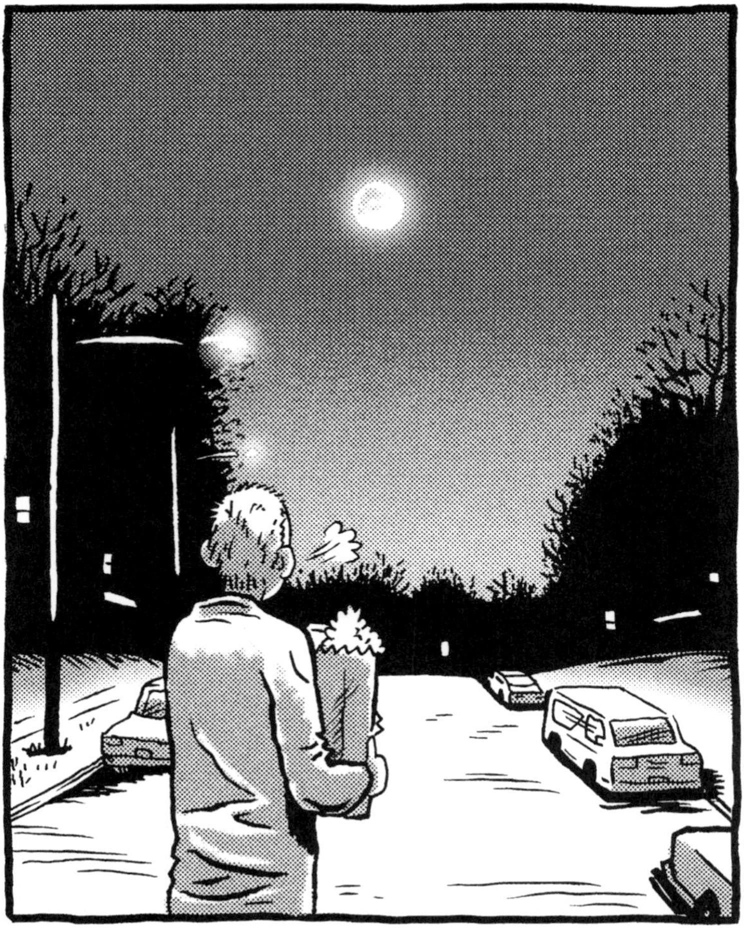

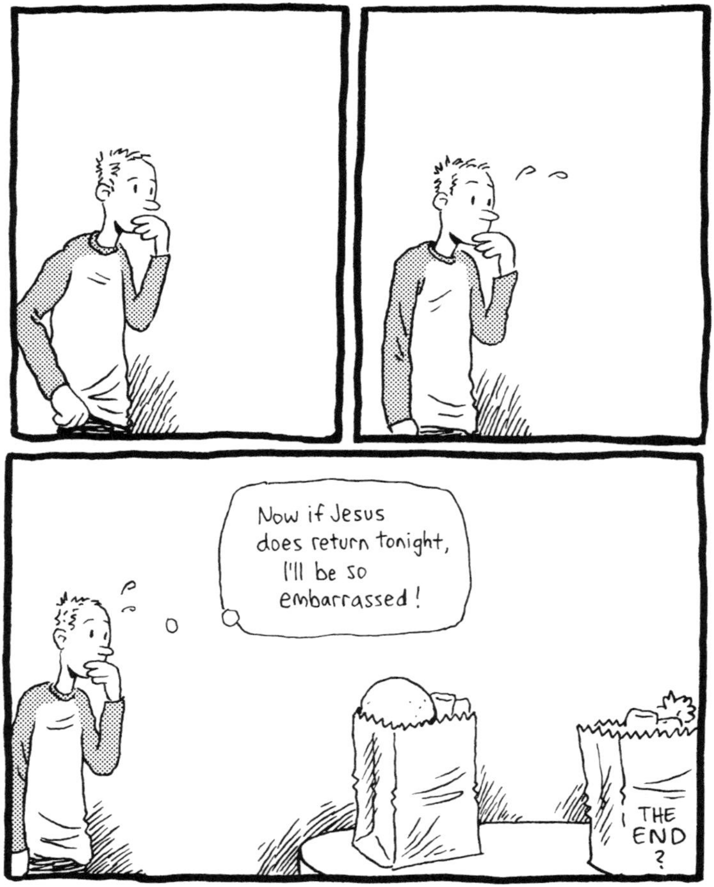
Now if Jesus does return tonight, I'll be so embarrassed!
THE END ?

BASKETBALL

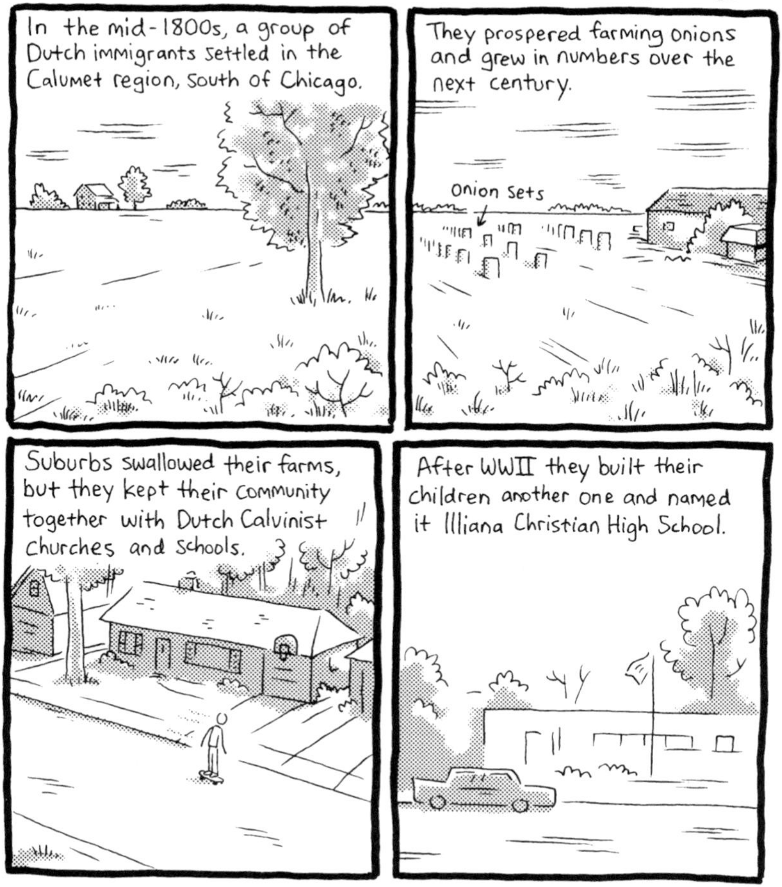
In the mid-1800s, a group of Dutch immigrants settled in the Calumet region, south of Chicago.
They prospered farming onions and grew in numbers over the next century.
onion sets
Suburbs swallowed their farms, but they kept their community together with Dutch Calvinist churches and schools.
After WWII they built their children another one and named it Illiana Christian High School.

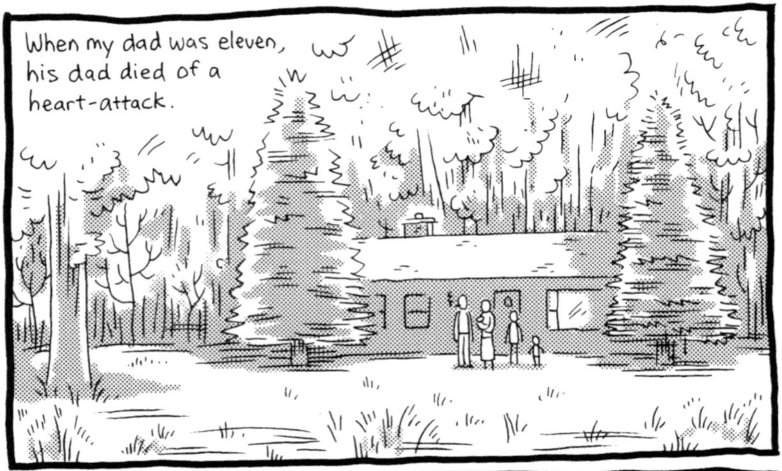
When my dad was eleven, his dad died of a heart-attack.

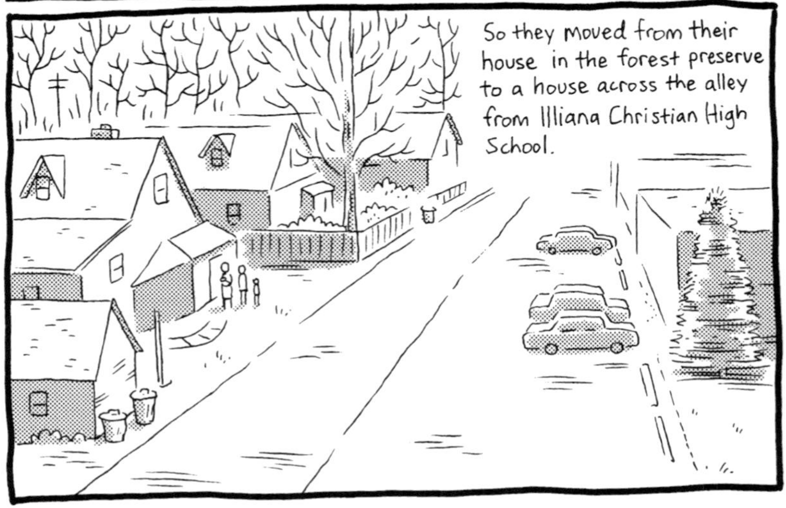
So they moved from their house in the forest preserve to a house across the alley from Illiana Christian High School.

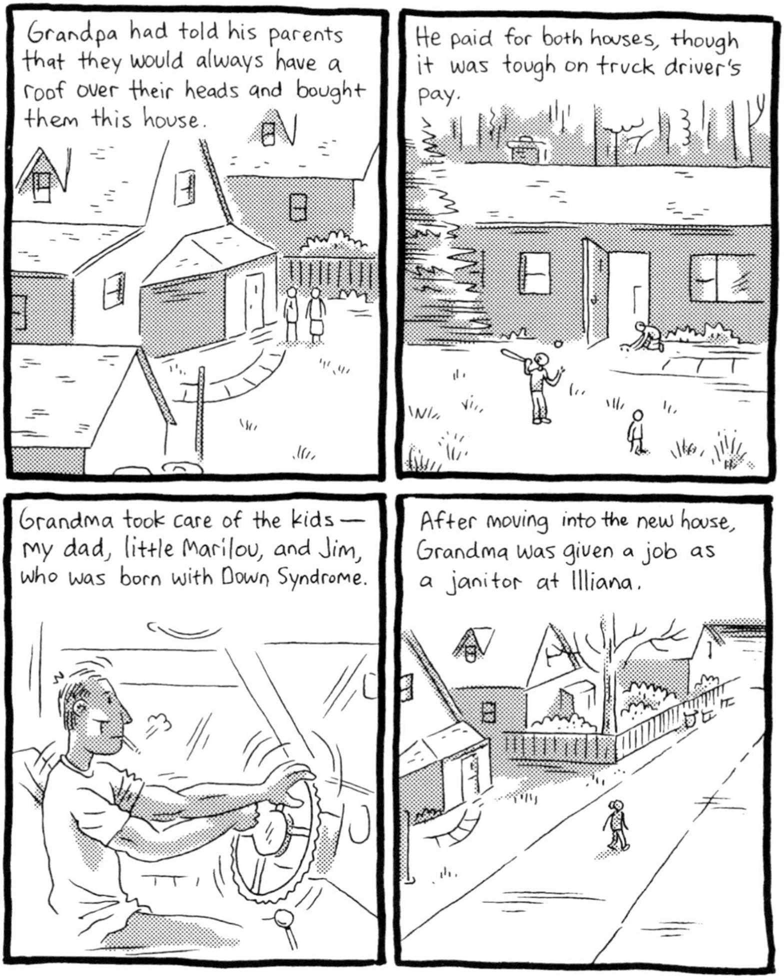
Grandpa had told his parents that they would always have a roof over their heads and bought them this house.
He paid for both houses, though it was tough on truck driver's pay.
Grandma took care of the kids — my dad, little Marilou, and Jim, who was born with Down Syndrome.
After moving into the new house, Grandma was given a job as a janitor at Illiana.

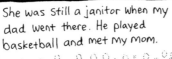
She was still a janitor when my dad went there. He played basketball and met my mom.

He loved basketball.

PSL Champs 19__

He would scrimmage at YMCAs in the city to learn. He would dunk.

He was offered scholarships, but he chose to go to college near home so he could help.

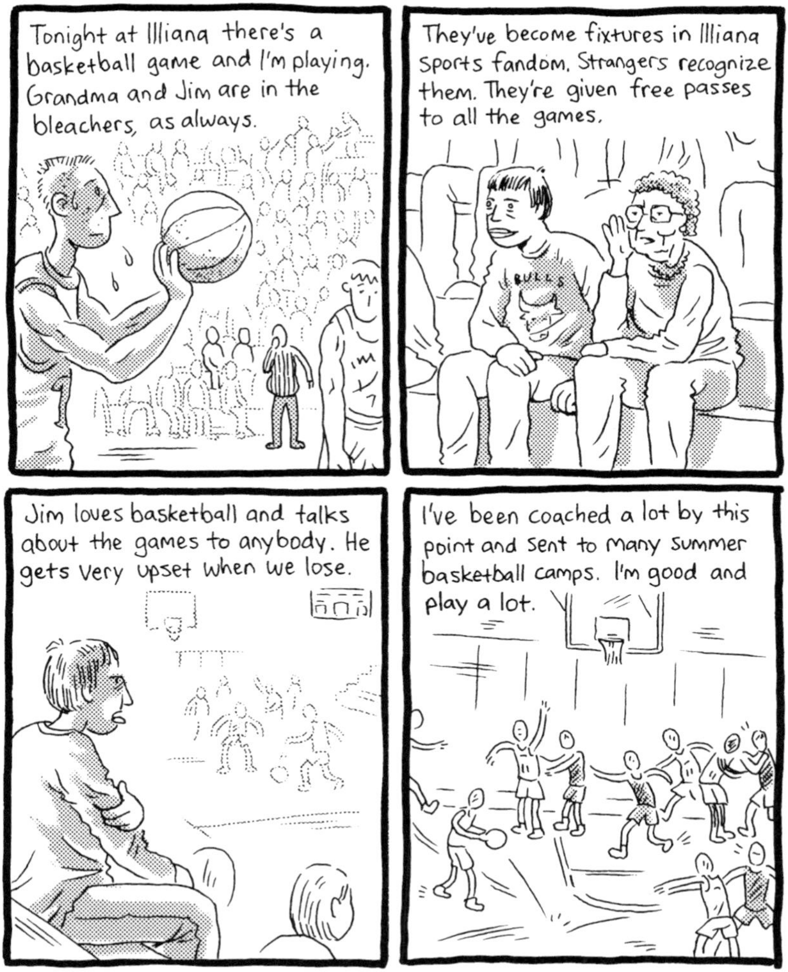
Tonight at Illiana there's a basketball game and I'm playing. Grandma and Jim are in the bleachers, as always.
JIM
They've become fixtures in Illiana sports fandom. Strangers recognize them. They're given free passes to all the games.
BULLS
Jim loves basketball and talks about the games to anybody. He gets very upset when we lose.
I've been coached a lot by this point and sent to many summer basketball camps. I'm good and play a lot.

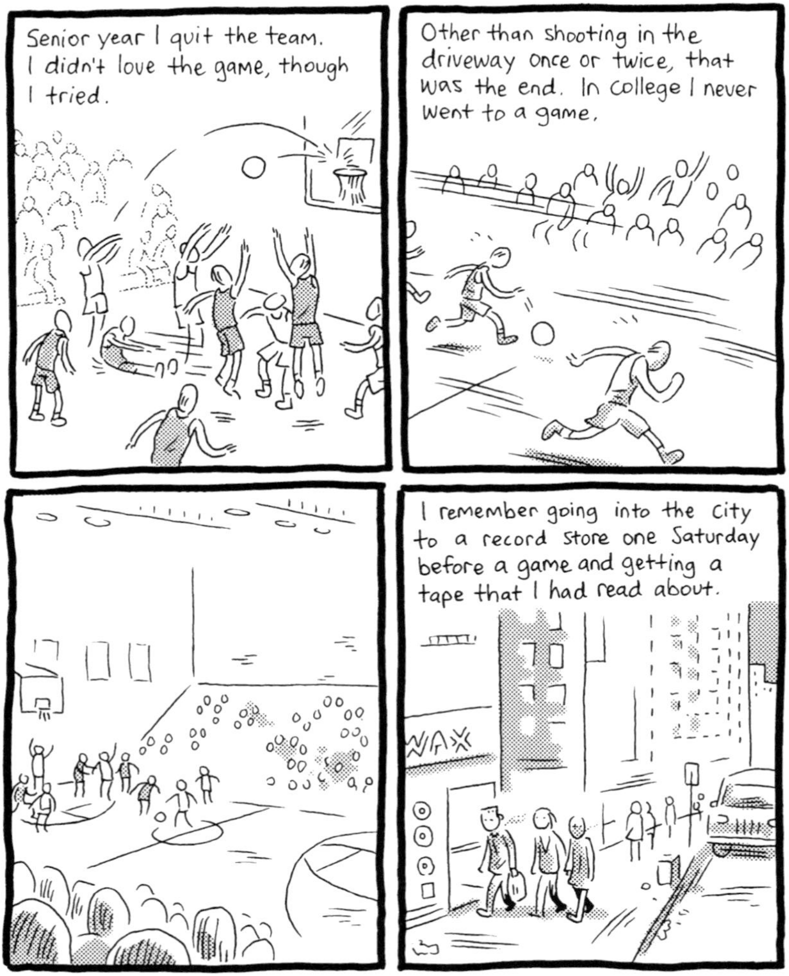
Senior year I quit the team. I didn't love the game, though I tried.
Other than shooting in the driveway once or twice, that was the end. In college I never went to a game.
I remember going into the city to a record store one Saturday before a game and getting a tape that I had read about.
WAX

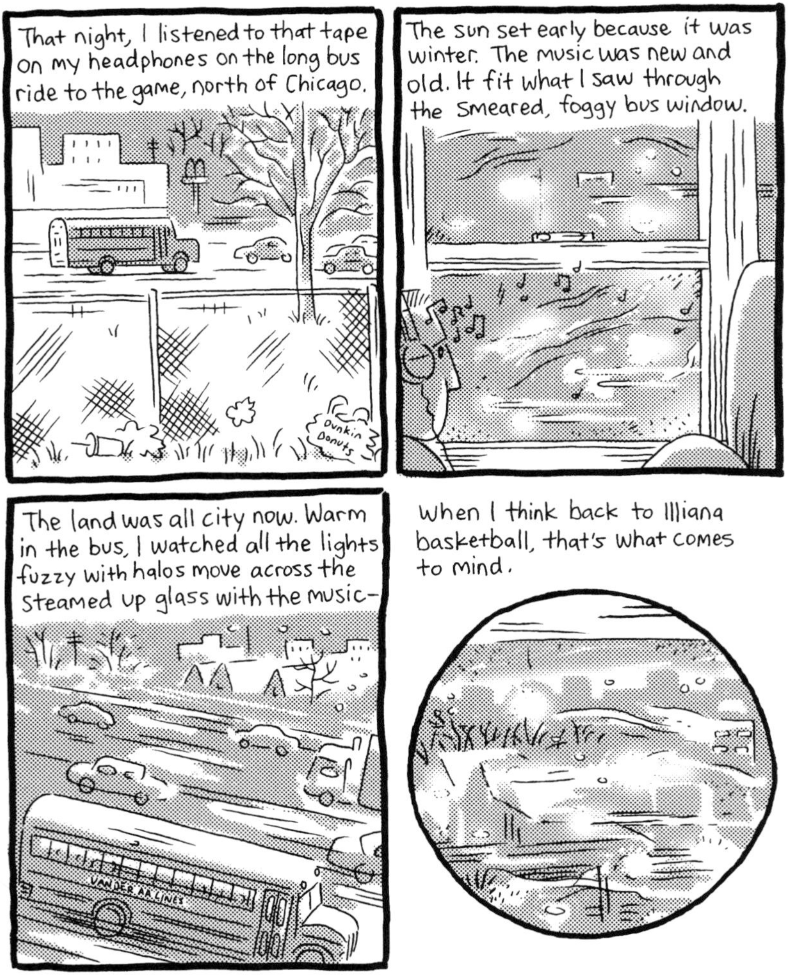
That night, I listened to that tape on my headphones on the long bus ride to the game, north of Chicago.
Dunkin Donuts
The sun set early because it was winter. The music was new and old. It fit what I saw through the smeared, foggy bus window.
The land was all city now. Warm in the bus, I watched all the lights fuzzy with halos move across the steamed up glass with the music-
VANDER AA LINES
When I think back to Illiana basketball, that's what comes to mind.

extras-->

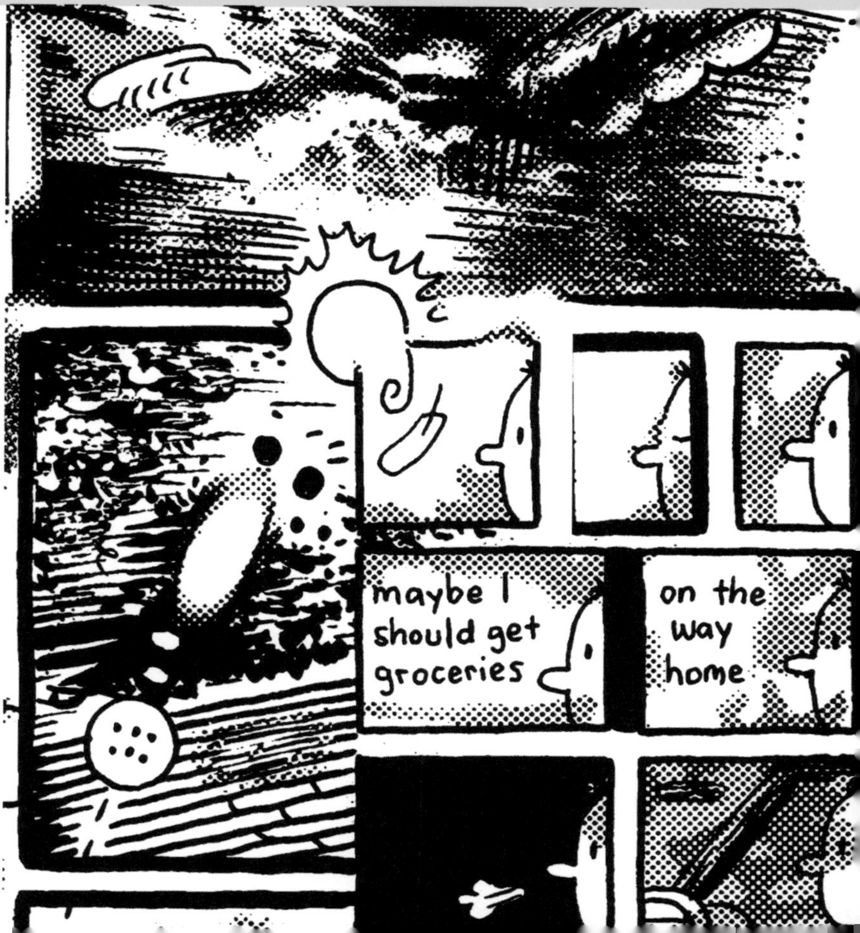
maybe I should get groceries
on the way home

the
sun
the
setting
sun
and the

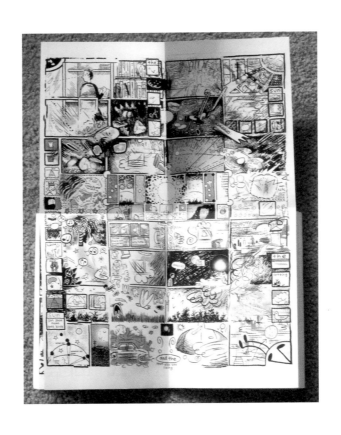

Original Fold-out, Supermonster #14

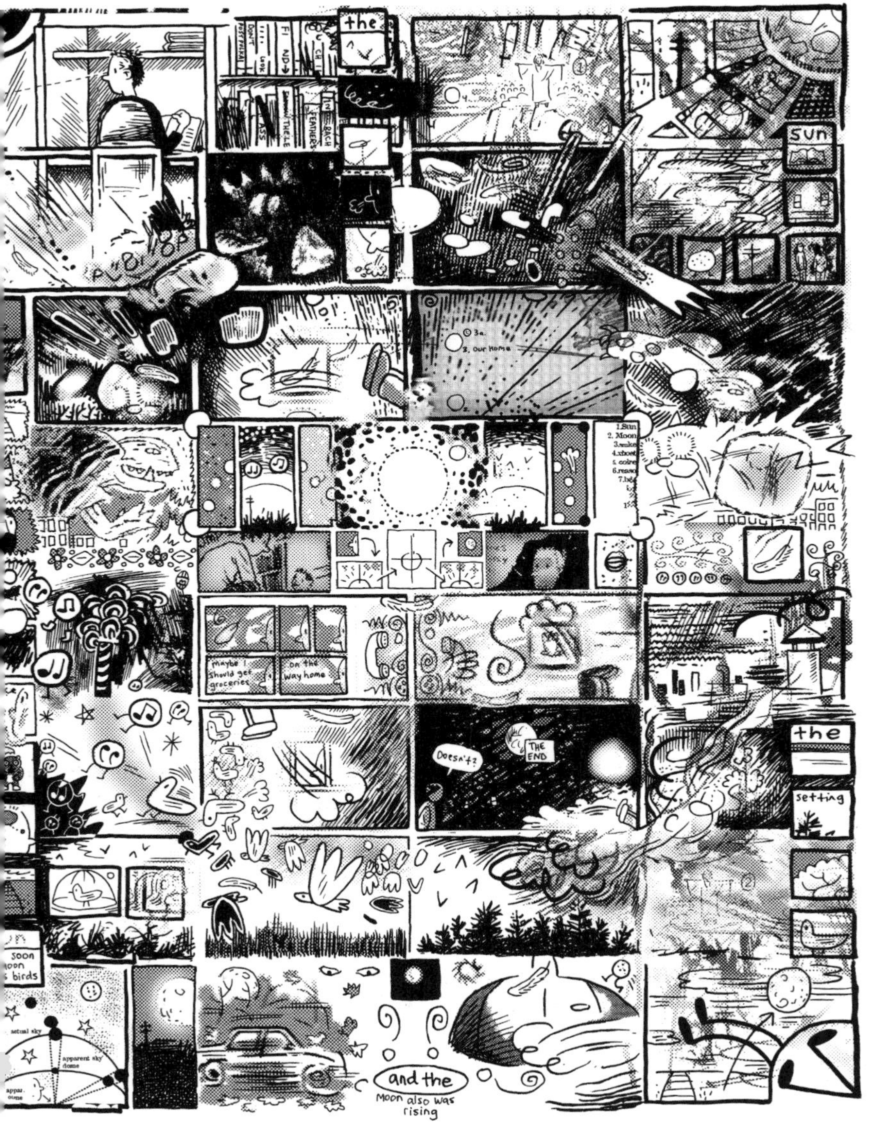

the
sun
3a.
3. our home
maybe I should get groceries
on the way home
Doesn't?
THE END
the
setting
actual sky
apparent sky dome
and the
Moon also was rising

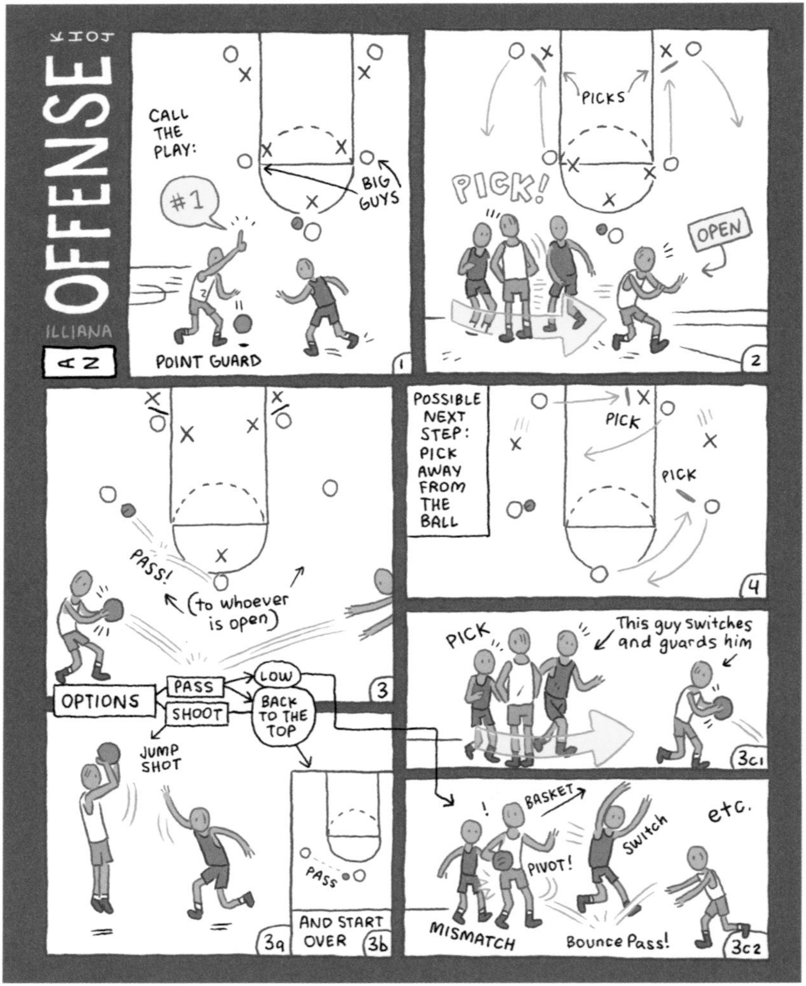
AN
OFFENSE
ILLIANA
CALL THE PLAY:
#1
BIG GUYS
POINT GUARD
1
PICKS
PICK!
OPEN
2
PASS!
(to whoever is open)
3
OPTIONS
PASS
SHOOT
LOW
BACK TO THE TOP
JUMP SHOT
3a
PASS
AND START OVER
3b
POSSIBLE NEXT STEP: PICK AWAY FROM THE BALL
PICK
PICK
4
PICK
This guy switches and guards him
3c1
BASKET
!
PIVOT!
Switch
etc.
MISMATCH
Bounce Pass!
3c2

Back cover, Or Else #2

Back cover, Supermonster #14

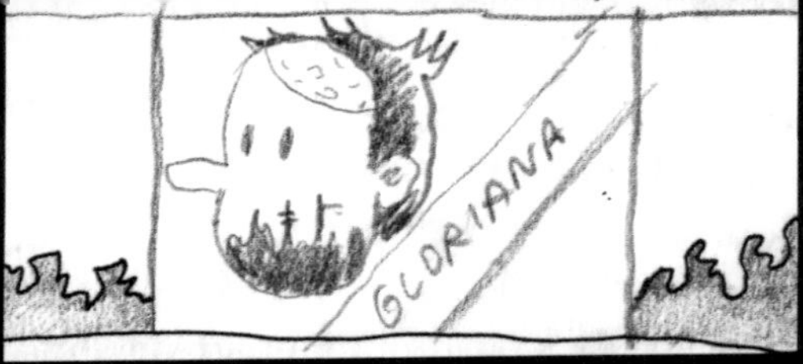
GLORIANA

INDEX

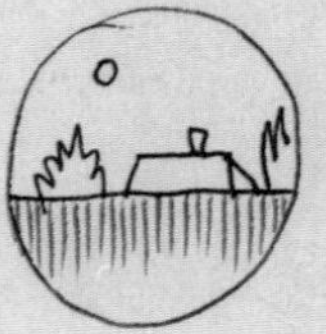

ABOUT THE AUTHOR

(pron. HIGH zing gah), St Louis, MO.
Wife + cat. ~~OTHER BOOKS~~

OTHER BOOKS AVAILABLE

kevinh@

→ Usscatastrophe.com

WILD KINGDOM

CURSES (stories)

MINI-COMIX

LEON BEYOND

(BLOGS)

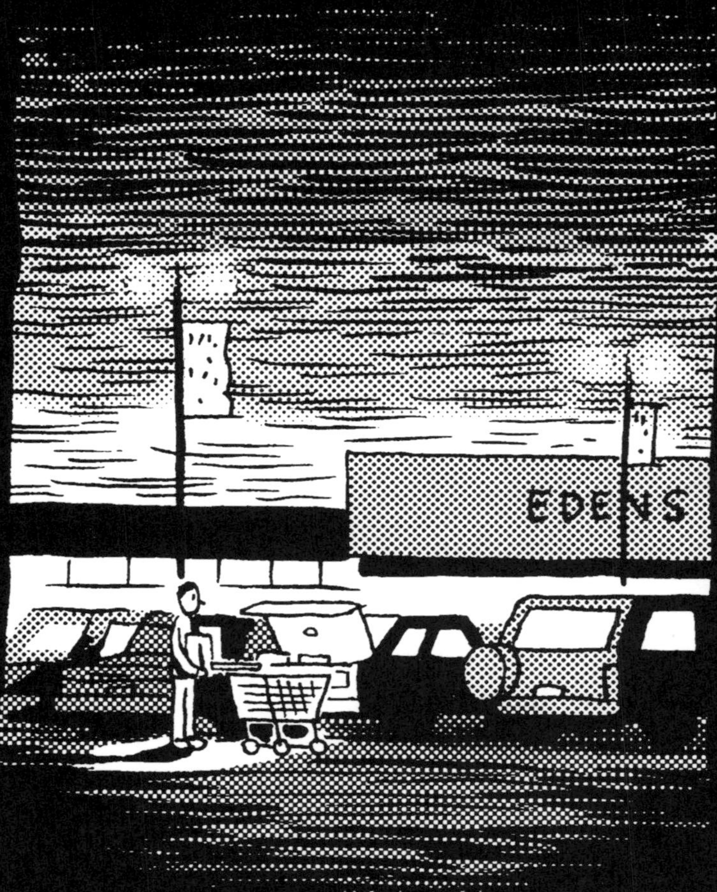
EDENS

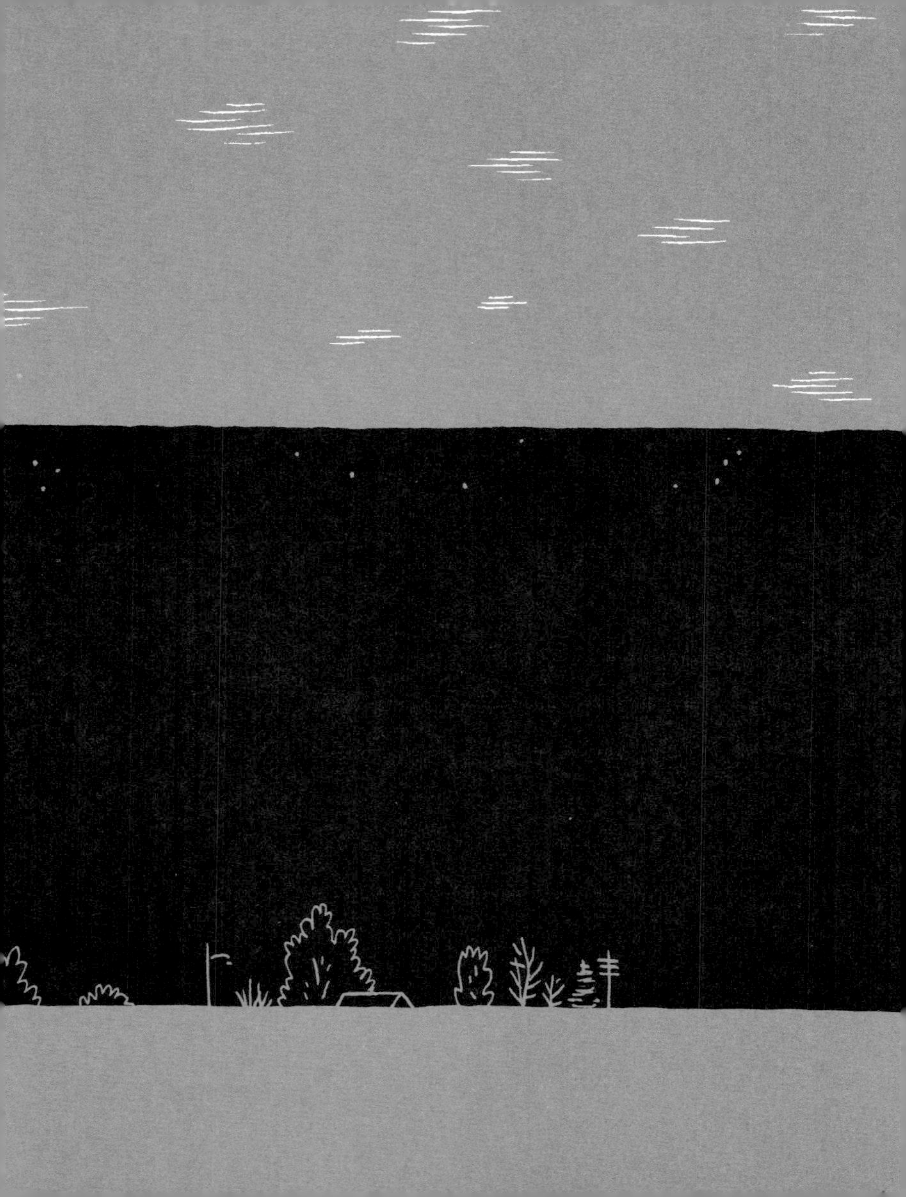